BIOLOGY
AND GEOLOGY
SECONDARY

BY ME

David Blanco Laserna
Elvira Chiquero Sanz
Andrew Critchley
Cassandra Gambill

LIFE ON EARTH

Contents

01 The biosphere

<< LOOKING BACK

- Which kingdoms do the organisms in the photos belong to?
- Which ones are able to make their own food?
- What do we call organisms that can't make their own food?
- What makes organisms A and B similar or different to the others?
- What makes up the biosphere?
- What are the differences between living and non-living things?

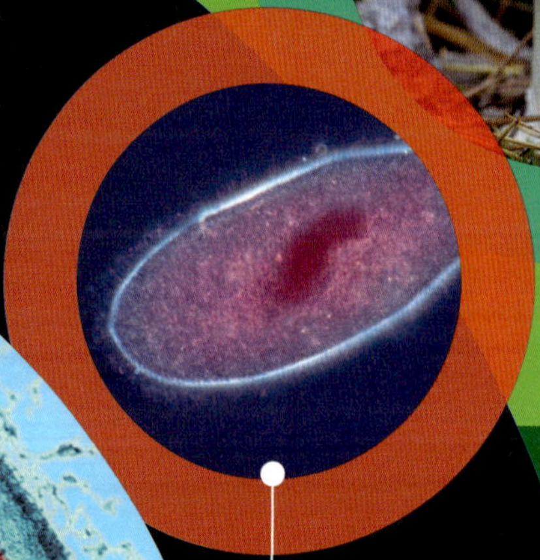

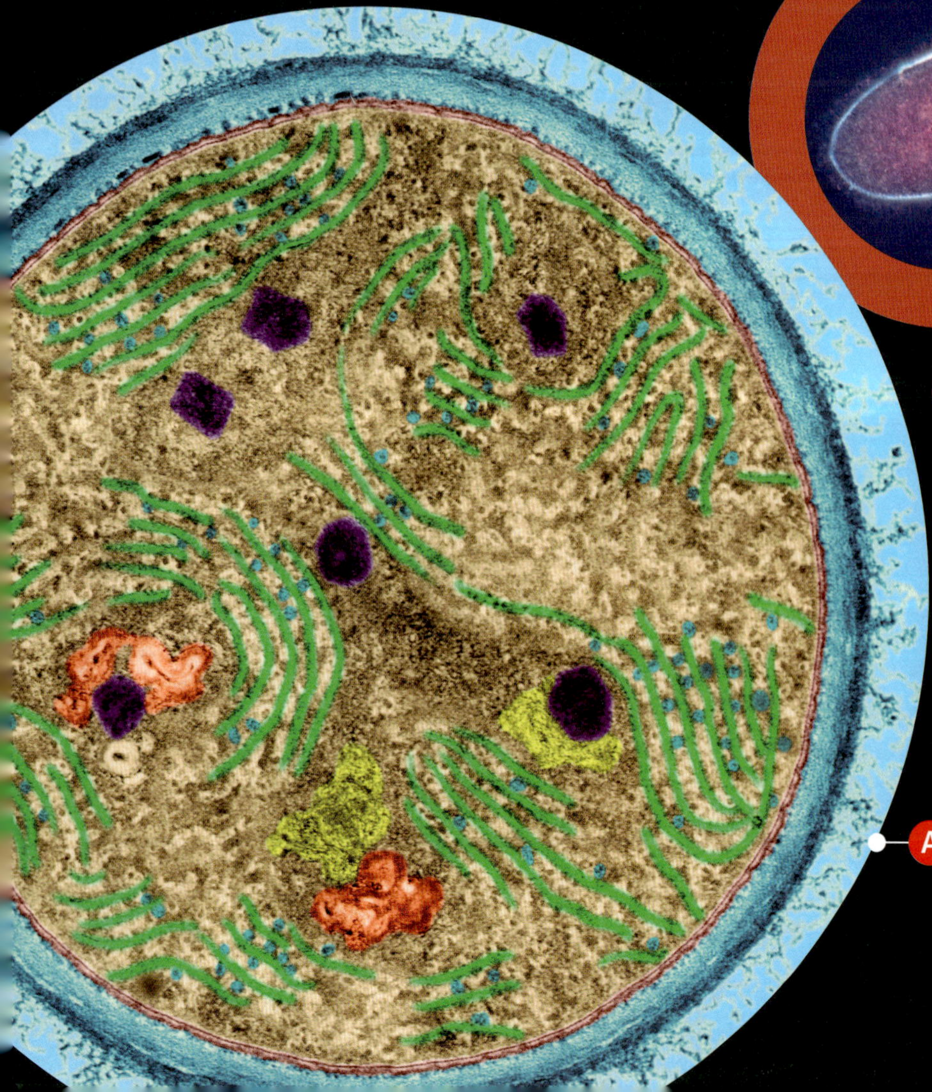

Living or non-living?

The air conditioner in my flat is a high-quality device. It uses electricity to work, but doesn't consume much energy because it is an energy-saving appliance. It also has a thermostat which detects temperature and humidity changes in the flat. If the temperature rises, the fans inside the device start moving automatically until it cools down again. Then it switches off. In addition, the device takes up very little space. It fits perfectly in a gap above the bookcase, where it's been for the past ten years.

A couple of days ago my air conditioner broke and I've just been told it can't be repaired. The new one I'm thinking of buying is okay too, but far bigger than the old one. It doesn't fit in the gap where the other one used to be!

- Which three characteristics of the air conditioner make it similar to a living thing?
- Does the air conditioner have any characteristics that make it different to a living thing?

Lotus flower

LOOKING FORWARD >>

- What allows Earth to support life?
- Which chemical elements make up living matter?
- Why is autotrophic nutrition so important?
- How many different types of cells are there?
- What is taxonomy?
- Which kingdoms include autotrophic organisms?
- What is a species?
- How do we name species?

1 Life on Earth

➲ What allows Earth to support life?

There is life almost everywhere on Earth, even in the most hostile and extreme environments, such as the ice sheet of Greenland and the Atacama Desert – the driest place on the planet.

The **biosphere** is the sum of all living things on the planet and the physical environment in which they live.

The biosphere is an **uneven** layer that extends from the bottom of the sea to the tops of the highest mountains. It is not only irregular in **thickness**, but also in diversity. This means that we can find a wide variety of life in a few square metres of rainforest, but we would need to walk for kilometres to find any sign of life in a desert.

1.1 How is life on Earth possible?

The Earth is unique in the Universe because it is the only planet where life is known to exist. The following **factors** make life on Earth possible:

Optimal distance from the Sun and, therefore, **optimal temperature.** The Earth is 150 million kilometres from the Sun. This distance means that the amount of light and heat the planet receives is suitable for living things.

Presence of oxygen and carbon dioxide in the atmosphere. Most living things need oxygen to live. On Earth, oxygen is produced by algae, some bacteria and plants through photosynthesis. Carbon dioxide is needed during this process.

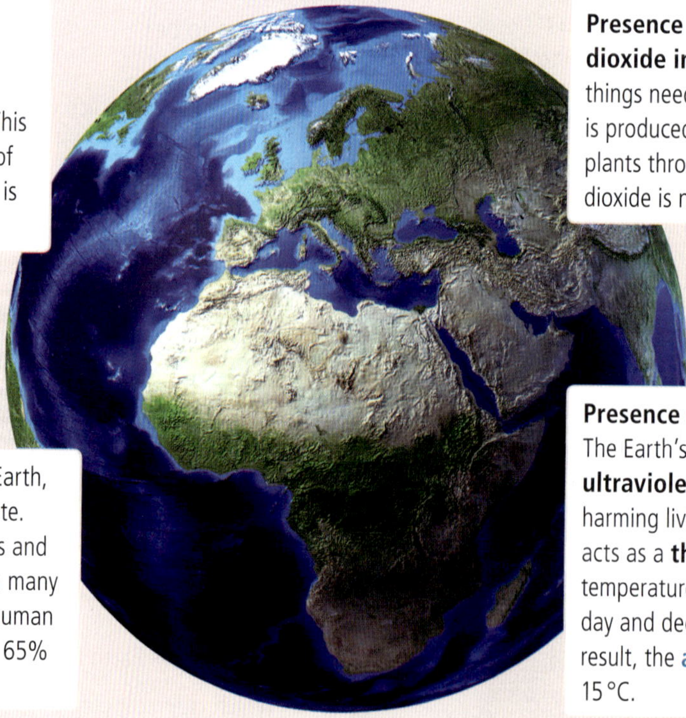

Presence of liquid water. On Earth, most of the water is in a liquid state. Water is essential for all organisms and it is also the environment in which many of them live. Remember that the human body is made up of approximately 65% water.

Presence of a protective atmosphere. The Earth's atmosphere filters the Sun's **ultraviolet rays,** stopping them from harming living things. The atmosphere also acts as a **thermal controller.** It stops the temperature increasing too much during the day and decreasing too much at night. As a result, the **average** temperature on Earth is 15 °C.

ACTIVITIES

1. Explain what we mean when we say that the biosphere is an *uneven* layer.
2. What do plants need sunlight for? Do all animals need sunlight too? Explain your answers.
3. Look for more information about how the atmosphere filters the Sun's ultraviolet rays.

2 What makes a living thing 'living'?

Which chemical elements make up living matter?

Both living and non-living things are made up of matter. However, all living things share certain **common characteristics** that distinguish them from non-living things. These characteristics can help us identify a mineral as a non-living thing and a butterfly as living.

NON-LIVING THINGS

Non-living things are made up of **inorganic matter**. The most abundant chemical elements which make up inorganic matter are: **oxygen (O)**, **silicon (Si)**, **aluminium (Al)** and **iron (Fe)**.

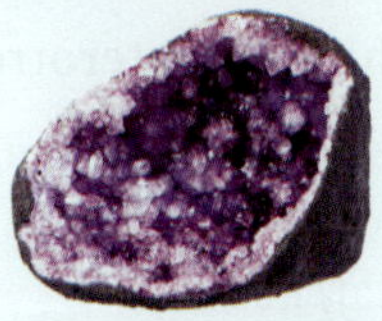

LIVING THINGS

All living things, also called **organisms,** are made up of the same chemical elements. The elements that form part of living matter are known as **bioelements.**

The six most abundant bioelements are: **carbon (C)**, **hydrogen (H)**, **oxygen (O)**, **nitrogen (N)**, **phosphorus (P)** and **sulphur (S).** They make up more than 90% of living matter.

The atoms and molecules of bioelements combine with each other through chemical reactions, producing **biomolecules.** Biomolecules may be:

- **inorganic**, such as **water** and **mineral salts**.
- **organic** (unique to living things), such as **carbohydrates**, **lipids**, **proteins** and **nucleic acids**.

In order to classify something as living it must:

- be composed of **bioelements**.
- be made up of small units called **cells**.
- perform the three **vital functions** of **nutrition**, **reproduction** and **interaction**.
- **grow** and **develop**.
- **adapt** to its environment in order to survive.
- **move** in some way.

FUNCTION OF BIOMOLECULES

- **Water** is where reactions take place in organisms.
- **Carbohydrates** provide an energy source for the cells and may also play a structural role.
- **Lipids** function as an energy reserve and also contribute to cell structure.
- **Proteins** are needed for growth and the maintenance of body structures.
- **Nucleic acids** are responsible for holding genetic information.

ACTIVITIES

4. What characteristics do living and non-living things share? What makes them different? Show them in a Venn diagram.
5. Classify the following substances as bioelements or biomolecules: water, carbon, sugars, proteins, sulphur, oxygen, hydrogen, nitrogen, nucleic acids and mineral salts.
6. Search and find out which foods are high in:
   a. proteins
   b. carbohydrates
   c. lipids
7. What is DNA? Look for information on it and find out which biomolecules make it up.

3 Functions of living things

➲ Why is autotrophic nutrition so important?

The vital functions of nutrition, interaction and reproduction are common to all organisms on Earth despite their incredible diversity.

3.1 Nutrition

Nutrition enables organisms to obtain energy to perform activities such as growing and restoring damaged structures.

There are two types of nutrition: **autotrophic** and **heterotrophic**.

AUTOTROPHIC NUTRITION

Autotrophic organisms (**autotrophs**) capture energy from their environment and use it to transform inorganic substances, such as water, carbon dioxide and mineral salts, into organic matter. The process through which most autotrophs make their own food is called **photosynthesis**.

Plants, **algae** and some **bacteria** are autotrophs.

HETEROTROPHIC NUTRITION

Heterotrophic organisms (**heterotrophs**) cannot produce their own food. They obtain organic matter by feeding on other organisms. Heterotrophs depend on autotrophs and other heterotrophs in order to get the nutrients they need.

Animals, **protozoans** and **fungi** are heterotrophs.

Heterotrophs can:

- obtain energy from eating plants (**herbivores**).
- obtain energy from eating other animals (**carnivores**).
- eat both plants and animals (**omnivores**).
- obtain nutrients from dead organic matter (**saprotrophs**). Fungi are saprotrophic organisms.

ACTIVITIES

8. Give an example of a carnivore, a herbivore, a saprotroph, an omnivore and an autotroph. Which ones can make their own food?
9. What is the relationship between the two types of nutrition?
10. Imagine that a meteorite hit the Earth and caused a dust cloud that prevented sunlight from reaching the Earth's surface. Why do you think this would lead to the extinction of some groups of living things?

3.2 Interaction

Interaction is the ability of organisms to obtain information about the changes in their environment and their own organism, and to adapt to these changes.

Changes in the environment of an organism, such as changes in temperature and humidity, or in the organism itself, such as hunger, are called **stimuli**. The adaptations or the reactions to those changes are called **responses**. Responses can vary considerably.

In animals, a response can be a sudden movement of the muscles.

In plants, a response can be a slow movement towards the Sun in search of sunlight.

DID YOU KNOW?

Worker bees use sight and smell to identify the colours and smells of nectar and pollen-rich flowers. When they find a food source, they return to the beehive and tell the other bees where it can be found. They communicate this information using very precise movements known as the **waggle dance**. Austrian scientist Karl von Frisch made this discovery, for which he received a Nobel Prize.

What are the benefits of bee pollen to humans?

3.3 Reproduction

Reproduction is the capacity of organisms to form new individuals similar to themselves. It can be asexual or sexual.

ASEXUAL REPRODUCTION

Two or more identical individuals are produced from a single one.

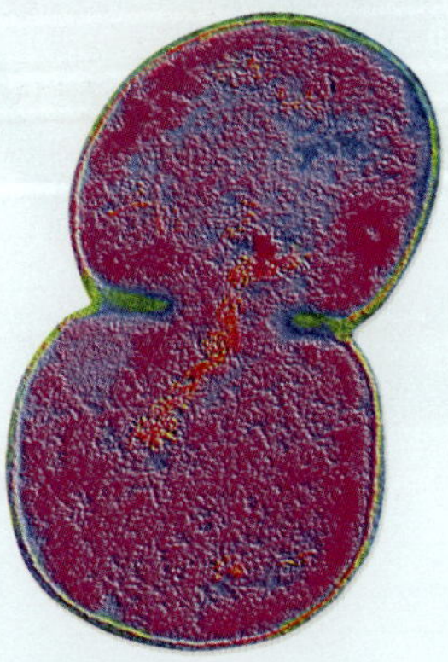

Cell division in bacteria

SEXUAL REPRODUCTION

Two individuals of different sexes are required. These organisms produce specialised cells known as **gametes**. These gametes join together to produce new organisms which are similar, but not identical, to their progenitors.

Starfish usually reproduce sexually but some starfish can also reproduce asexually. If a starfish's arm is cut off and it keeps a part of the centre of the body, a whole new starfish can form from the removed arm. A starfish can also regenerate a new arm to replace the lost one.

ACTIVITIES

11. What do living organisms perceive through the function of interaction?

12. How do you think living things usually respond when they feel threatened?

13. All organisms eventually die. Which vital function ensures the survival of a species?

4 Cells: the units of life

All living things are composed of one or more cells, each capable of carrying out the functions of life. All cells come from pre-existing cells.

According to the number of cells, organisms can be single-celled or multicellular. **Single-celled** or **unicellular organisms**, such as bacteria or protozoans, are made up of just one cell. **Multicellular organisms**, such as human beings, are made up of a large number of cells.

4.1 Types of cells

Based on their complexity, there are two types of cells: **prokaryotic** cells and **eukaryotic** cells.

PROKARYOTIC CELLS

This is the simplest type of cell. *Prokaryotic* means 'before a nucleus'. This is because prokaryotic cells do not have a defined nucleus and the DNA is dispersed in the cytoplasm. This is the cell type found in single-celled organisms such as **bacteria**.

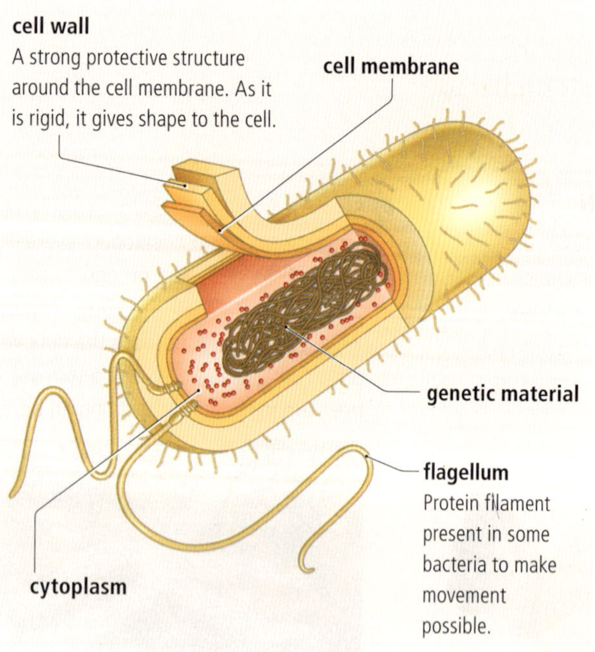

EUKARYOTIC CELLS

Eukaryotic literally means 'with a true nucleus'. In these cells, the genetic material is protected by a double membrane that separates it from the cytoplasm. Eukaryotic cells are more complex than prokaryotic cells because they have specialised organelles. These organelles play different roles in the cell.

ANIMAL CELL

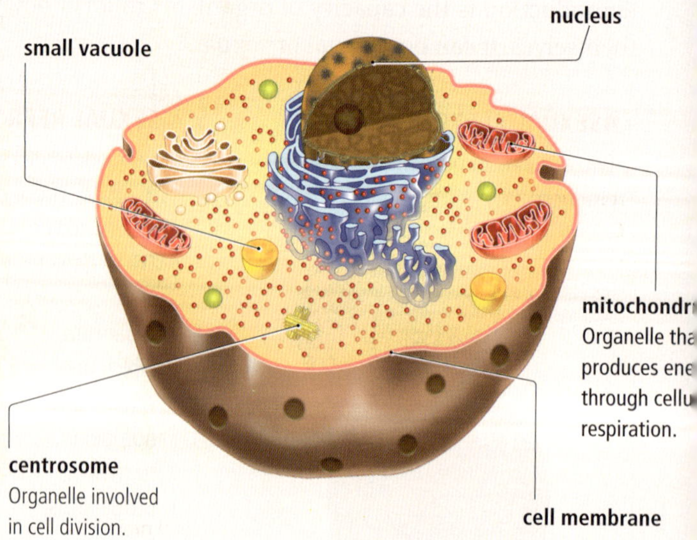

ACTIVITIES

14. Which part of a prokaryotic cell contains genetic material?

15. A tumour appears when cells don't die when they should and new cells form that the body doesn't need. Which part of the cell is responsible for this uncontrolled growth? Justify your answer.

16. Explain the literal meaning of *prokaryotic* and *eukaryotic*. Make drawings to explain the two terms.

17. If you're injured, which cellular vital function will repair your damaged tissues? Explain your answer.

18. Which kind of cells are the simplest? Explain why.

How many different types of cells are there?

These two cell types have three common parts:

- **Cell membrane.** A **covering** which surrounds and protects the cell and controls the passage of substances in and out of it.
- **Cytoplasm.** A **viscous** liquid which fills the inside of the cell and in which chemical reactions take place. In eukaryotic cells, the cytoplasm contains different types of **organelles.**
- **Genetic material.** This is made up of deoxyribonucleic acid (**DNA**), which contains the information that directs and controls the functions of the cell. This material also determines an organism's characteristics and is passed from the parent organisms to their offspring.

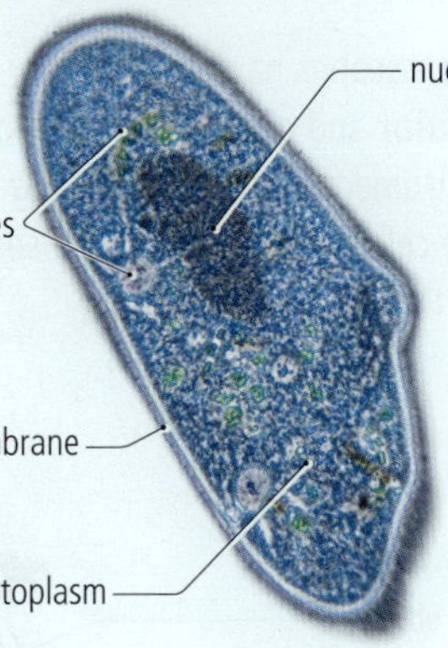

Parts of a cell

There are two types of eukaryotic cells:

animal cells found in protozoans and animals.

plant cells found in algae and plants.

Animal cells and plant cells have some organelles in common. They also have their own specific organelles, such as **centrosomes** in animal cells, and **cell walls** and **chloroplasts** in plant cells.

PLANT CELL

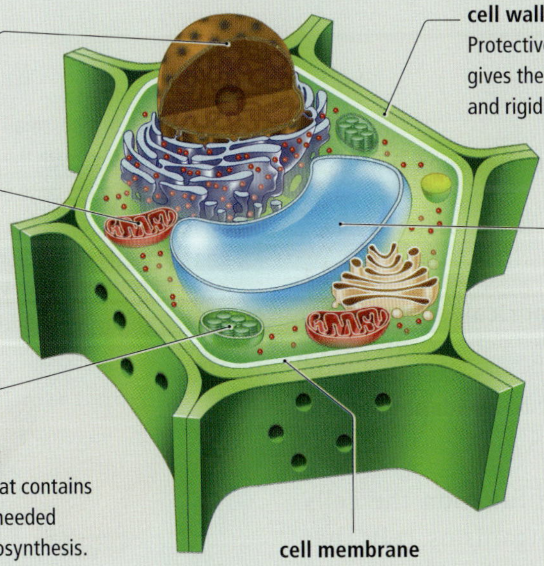

DID YOU KNOW?

There are more cells in one human body (approximately 60 trillion cells) than galaxies in the whole Universe. Even when an organism stops growing, its cells carry on dividing in order to **replace** the cells that have died. Does everybody have the same amount of cells in their body?

19. Explain the differences between an animal cell and a plant cell.

20. Which part of a plant cell contains chlorophyll?

21. Choose the right ending for the sentence and explain why.

Our body grows bigger by increasing *the size of the cells/the number of cells*.

4.2 The discovery of cells

THE MICROSCOPE

Microscopes have two lenses: **ocular** and **objective**. This optical instrument magnifies the image of the cells so that they can be seen by the **naked eye**.

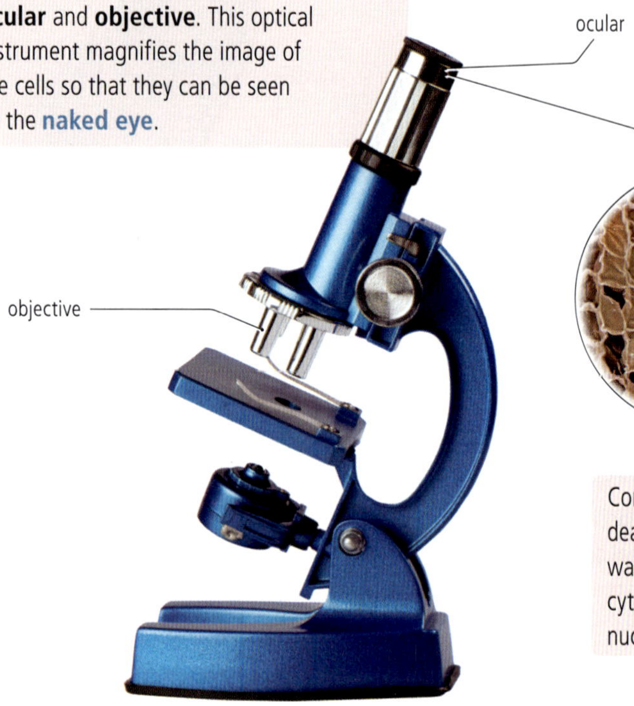

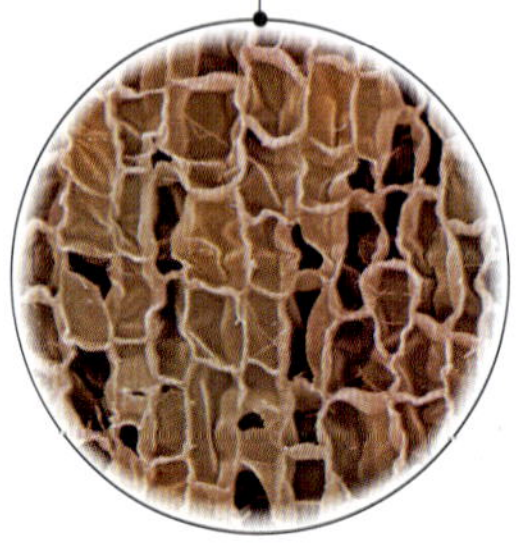

Cork is made up of dead cells with cell walls but without cytoplasm or a nucleus.

- In 1665, the English naturalist **Robert Hooke** (1635–1703) viewed a thin slice of cork under a very basic microscope. He observed what appeared to be tiny empty spaces, which he called **cells** (from the Latin word *cella*, meaning 'small room').
- Later, the Dutch textile merchant **Anton van Leeuwenhoek** (1632–1723) built a **rudimentary** microscope which he used to observe microscopic organisms that he called 'animalcules'.
- The development of the microscope and other research methods led to the conclusion that cells are the smallest units that make up a living thing. Later observations **revealed** that cells are not empty and that it is possible to observe structures and organelles inside them.

4.3 Size and form of cells

The size of cells varies a lot, although most cells measure between 5 and 50 microns.

$$1 \text{ micron } (\mu) = 0.001\text{mm}$$

Cells come in a wide variety of shapes: spherical, cylindrical, star-shaped, polygonal, disc-like and many more.

- In single-celled organisms, shape is related to how they have adapted to the environment in which they live.
- In multicellular organisms, shape is related to the function the cells perform within the organism. In some multicellular organisms, cells that perform the same function group together, forming tissue.

DID YOU KNOW?

Most cells are so small that they can't normally be seen with the naked eye. Some cells, however, are large enough to be seen without the aid of optical instruments. You can find the most common example in your own fridge! Did you know that each chicken egg is a single **unfertilised** egg cell?

ACTIVITIES

22. What are the shapes of the cells in the photos?

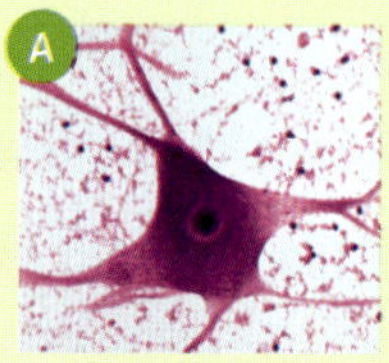

Neuron

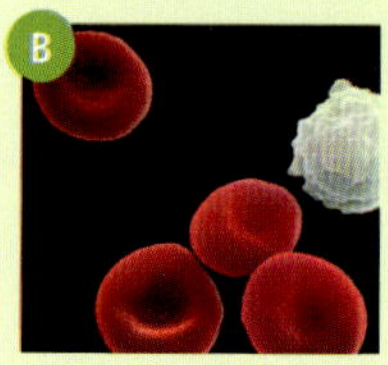

Red blood cells

Leaf cells

23. Look for information about the functions of the cells in Activity 22. Write a short report.
24. Were they actually cells what Hooke observed using his microscope? Explain your answer.
25. Look for information and find out what cork is and where it comes from.

5 Classifying organisms

What is taxonomy?

In order to better understand the relationship between organisms, we **classify** them. This means that we group organisms together based on their common characteristics. Some are closely related, while others share very little in common.

5.1 Taxonomy

Taxonomy is the science of classifying organisms using a **hierarchical** system of classification.

There have been lots of **attempts** to classify living things throughout history. The **system of classification** we use today is based on the hierarchical system created by Swedish botanist **Carl Linnaeus** (1707–1778). Linnaeus' system was called **binomial nomenclature.**

Organisms are classified into groups called **taxa** (singular **taxon**). The seven taxonomic levels from the largest to the smallest are: **kingdom, phylum, class, order, family, genus** and **species.**

Below you can see how you, as a human, are classified.

ALL LIVING THINGS

- **kingdom:** animals — The Animal Kingdom includes several phyla.
- **phylum:** chordates — In addition to mammals, the chordate phylum also includes fish, amphibian, reptile and bird classes.
- **class:** mammals — Whales, dolphins, bats, platypuses and kangaroos belong to different orders of the mammal class.
- **order:** primates — The primate order includes other families of animals, such as lemurs, monkeys and great apes.
- **family:** hominids
- **genus:** *homo* — *Homo sapiens* is the only surviving species of the *Homo* genus.
- **species:** *homo sapiens*

YOU

BIG THINKER

Carl Linnaeus, called the father of taxonomy, was born in 1707, the eldest of five children. His father, Nils, was a keen gardener who taught Carl botany. In fact, at school, Carl was often more interested in memorising plant names than in listening to the teacher. By the age of five, Carl had his own garden.

Which of your hobbies require you to memorise things?

ACTIVITIES

26. What taxon contains the largest number of different species of living things? Justify your answers.

a. a phylum or a family

b. an order or a class

c. a genus or a kingdom

d. a genus or a family

27. Decide if the sentences are true and explain your answer.

a. An order is subdivided into several classes.

b. A phylum is subdivided into several orders.

28. Look for more information about other primates apart from hominids. Choose three families of primates and write a short report about them.

6 The five kingdoms

Which kingdoms include autotrophic organisms?

Lynn Margulis (1938–2011) was an American biologist who proposed the classification of organisms into **five kingdoms**: **Monera**, **Protoctista**, **Fungus**, **Plant** and **Animal**. This is one of the most widely accepted classifications of living things.

MONERANS

- Monerans are prokaryotic, single-celled organisms.
- They can be autotrophs or heterotrophs.
- They reproduce asexually.
- They are primarily **bacteria**.

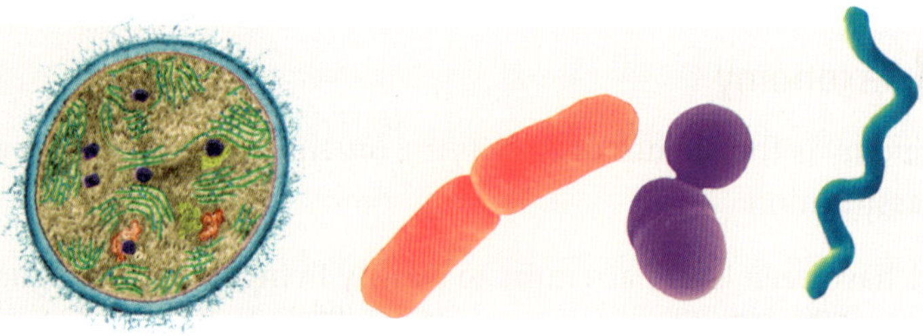

PROTOCTISTS

- Protoctists are eukaryotic organisms. They can be single-celled or multicellular.
- They can be autotrophs, such as **algae** that perform photosynthesis, or heterotrophs, such as **protozoans**.
- They reproduce sexually and asexually.

FUNGI

- Fungi are eukaryotic organisms. They can be single-celled, such as **yeasts**, or multicellular, such as **mushrooms** and **moulds**.
- They are heterotrophs.
- They reproduce sexually and asexually.
- They can't move from one place to another.

PLANTS

- Plants are eukaryotic, multicellular organisms.
- They are autotrophs.
- They reproduce sexually and asexually.
- They carry out photosynthesis.
- They can move, but not from one place to another.

ANIMALS

- Animals are eukaryotic, multicellular organisms.
- They are heterotrophs.
- They reproduce sexually and, in some cases, asexually.
- They have sense organs and can move around.

ACTIVITIES

29. In which kingdoms are all the organisms multicellular?
30. What are the differences between plants and fungi?
31. In which kingdoms are there heterotrophic organisms?

7 What is a species?

A species is a group of organisms that **resemble** each other and can reproduce with one another as well as have **fertile** descendants, which means that the descendants can also reproduce.

7.1 How do we name species?

Linnaeus' **binomial nomenclature** gives each species a **Latin** or **scientific name** composed of two terms (*binomial* literally means 'two names'), both of them written in italics.

The first name, with a capitalised first letter, identifies the **genus** to which the species belongs.

The second name identifies the **species** within the genus. It usually describes some characteristic of the organism (*sapiens* = wise).

Homo sapiens

(House) sparrow
Passer domesticus

(Common) mushroom
Agaricus bisporus

Sunflower
Helianthus annuus

Tiger *Panthera tigris*

Each species has only one scientific name accepted by speakers of all languages. However, there are different common names for each species, depending on the region, country, and language, which may lead to confusion.

DID YOU KNOW?

Domestic dogs are the most diverse-looking species of mammals. There are somewhere between 300 and 400 different **breeds** of domestic dogs, but all of them belong to just one species called *Canis familiaris*. All the different breeds can **mate** and have **viable** and fertile **puppies**.

Have you ever seen a mixed-breed dog?

ACTIVITIES

32. What is the advantage of scientific names of species over common names?

33. Explain whether the following sentence is true or false and why.

Breeds are groups of organisms within a species.

34. Domestic cats belong to the felidae family and their scientific name is *Felis catus*. All felids are carnivores. Look up the Latin names of other felids and their corresponding common names in a guide.

7.2 Biodiversity

According to the latest study, there are 8.7 million different species on Earth. The diversity of life on Earth is known as **biodiversity**.

Every organism on Earth **fulfills** a specific function in the planet's global ecosystem. This is why preserving biodiversity is so important.

Nowadays, many destructive human practices are damaging the planet's biodiversity, causing many species to become extinct.

ENDANGERED SPECIES

Endangered species or organisms are those which are under the threat of extinction.

There is a list of the world's endangered species, which is called the **Red List**. This list serves as a guide and determines the level of risk for different species.

Fifty percent of rainforest animal species are seriously endangered, the **mountain gorilla** being one of them. In Spain, the **Iberian imperial eagle** is also considered to be in danger of extinction.

Mountain gorilla

Iberian imperial eagle

ENDEMIC SPECIES

Some species are restricted to certain areas in the world while others are **widespread**.

An endemic species is one that can only be found in a particular region and nowhere else in the world.

The term 'endemic' could refer to an animal, a plant, a fungus, or even a microorganism. Endemic species are often endangered.

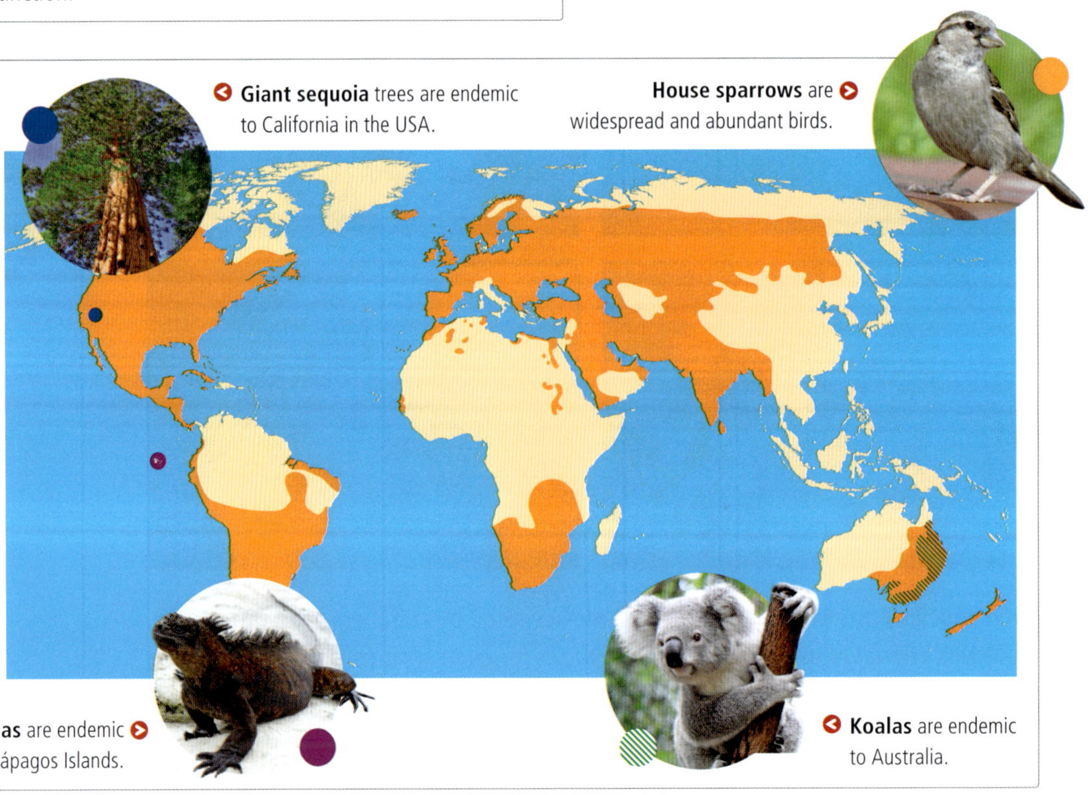

Giant sequoia trees are endemic to California in the USA.

House sparrows are widespread and abundant birds.

Marine Iguanas are endemic to the Galápagos Islands.

Koalas are endemic to Australia.

ACTIVITIES

35. Why do you think it is so important to protect and preserve biodiversity?

36. Look for information and make a list of human activities that are causing a loss of biodiversity.

37. Do some research and decide whether the following organisms are endangered species, endemic species or both: the Mediterranean monk seal, the Iberian lynx, the Madagascan lemur, the Arizona agave. Where can each species be found?

Discovery techniques

TAXONOMY BEFORE AND AFTER LINNAEUS

How do we name species?

"Before Linnaeus, plants were given names that were expansively descriptive. The common ground cherry was called *Physalis amno ramosissime ramis angulosis glabris foliis dentoserratis*. Linnaeus lopped it back to *Physalis angulata*, which name it still uses. [...] A botanist could not be sure if *Rosa sylvestris alba cum rubore, folio glabro* was the same plant that others called *Rosa sylvestris inodora seu canina*. Linnaeus solved the puzzlement by calling it simply *Rosa canina*. [...]

The Linnaeus system is so well established that we can hardly imagine an alternative, but before Linnaeus, systems of classification were often highly whimsical. Animals might be categorized by whether they were thought handsome and noble or of no consequence. [Others] arranged [their] animals by their utility to man. Anatomical considerations barely came into it. Linnaeus made it his life's work to rectify this deficiency by classifying all that was alive according to its physical attributes. Taxonomy – which is to say the science of classification – has never looked back."

Bill Bryson
A Short History of Nearly Everything
Transworld Publishers

ACTIVITIES

1. What is the text about? Think of a different title for the text.
2. Look up the meaning of the following words in a dictionary: *to lop back, botanist, puzzlement, alternative, whimsical, barely, to come into, rectify, deficiency, attributes.*
3. Explain the criteria used to classify organisms:
   a. before Linnaeus
   b. since Linnaeus
4. What are the seven taxonomic levels from the largest to the smallest?
5. Explain what 'binomial nomenclature' means.
6. Give two examples of binomial nomenclature that appear in the text. What are the common names of these species?
7. Imagine you are an entomologist (a person who studies insects) and you've recently discovered three new species of butterfly of the genus *Buttercolouris*.

   a. Give each species a scientific name and a common name. Which name would be more useful and why?
   b. What criteria have you used to name them? Explain your decisions.

Revision activities

1. Imagine astronomers have recently discovered a new planet in a faraway galaxy and they are wondering whether it is likely to support life. Make a list of the characteristics this planet would need to sustain life as it is known on Earth.

2. Define biosphere and biodiversity. Is there more biodiversity in a desert or in a rainforest? Explain why.

3. Would life on Earth be possible in the following situations? Explain why in each case.
   - a. If water only existed in a solid state.
   - b. If all the algae and plants on Earth became extinct.
   - c. If the Earth were much closer to the Sun.
   - d. If there wasn't an atmosphere.

4. What are the characteristics shared by all living organisms?

5. Indicate the type of nutrition of the following organisms. Which ones are able to make their own food?
   - a. toadstool
   - b. wolf
   - c. palm tree
   - d. bacterium
   - e. protozoa
   - f. seaweed

6. Indicate the differences between each pair of terms or concepts:
   - a. biosphere and biodiversity
   - b. inorganic matter and organic matter
   - c. bioelements and biomolecules
   - d. sexual and asexual reproduction
   - e. interaction in animals and interaction in plants
   - f. unicellular and multicellular organisms
   - g. living and non-living things
   - h. endemic species and widespread species
   - i. carnivores and saprotrophs

7. Make sentences that use all the words in each group.
   - a. biomolecules, carbohydrates, organic
   - b. autotrophic, protoctists, heterotrophic
   - c. prokaryotic cells, genetic material, eukaryotic cells
   - d. biodiversity, risk, endangered species
   - e. cell wall, eukaryotic cells, animal cells

8. Briefly explain what a threatened species is and give three examples. Why is it so important to maintain our planet's biodiversity?

9. Say whether the following statements are true or false and correct the false ones:
   - a. Only bacteria reproduce asexually.
   - b. Individuals produced by sexual reproduction are identical to their progenitors.
   - c. Sexual reproduction takes place through the union of reproductive cells called gametes.
   - d. Individuals produced by asexual reproduction are identical to their progenitors.

10. Briefly explain the contribution of the following scientists to science. Why was their work so important?
    - a. Lynn Margulis
    - b. Carl Linnaeus
    - c. Robert Hooke

11. Find out which forms of life exist in the following extreme environments:
    - a. the ice sheet of Greenland
    - b. the Atacama desert
    - c. the Rio Tinto in Huelva

12. What is the process by which plants and algae produce their own food? Where do they get the energy for that process?

13. Look at the photos and identify the living things in them.

A

B

   - a. Which kingdom do the organisms in the photos belong to?
   - b. What environment do they live in?
   - c. Give examples of other groups of organisms that belong to the same kingdom.
   - d. Compare the two organisms in a Venn diagram. Show the characteristics they share and the ones that are specific to each one.

14 Write a short text about microscopes. It should include the following points:

- discovery
- parts
- types
- usefulness

15 A **mnemonic** is a small phrase or word that helps us to remember lists of important information. Here is an easy way to remember the classification of living things:

King Phillip Came Over From Great Spain

a. What do the letters stand for?

b. Say whether the rule organises the groups from the lowest to the highest or vice versa.

c. Which group contains the largest number of organisms? Which contains the smallest?

d. Create a mnemonic rule of your own to remember the same list.

16 Identify the kingdoms of the following organisms and give an example of each:

a. eukaryotic multicellular autotrophs

b. prokaryotic single-celled organisms

c. single-celled or multicellular heterotrophs

17 What two conditions are needed for organisms to belong to the same species?

18 Identify the kingdoms the organisms in the photos belong to. Write a short text about each one including the following information:

a. type of cells that make them up

b. single-celled or multicellular

c. type of nutrition

d. aquatic or terrestrial

e. other characteristics you might consider important

19 How can we classify cells based on their complexity? Give examples of organisms with each type of cell.

20 In your notebook, complete the following Venn diagrams. Show the characteristics and structures that the different types of cells share and the ones that are specific to each one.

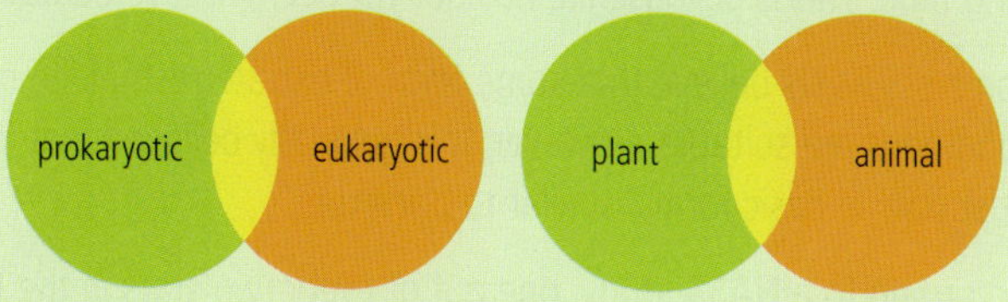

21 Indicate the type of cell and label the pictures.

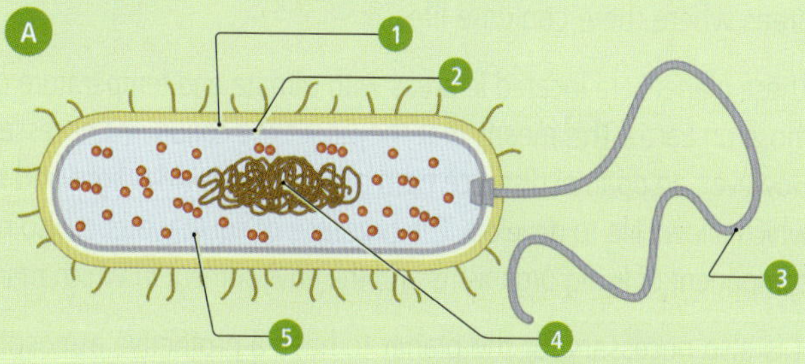

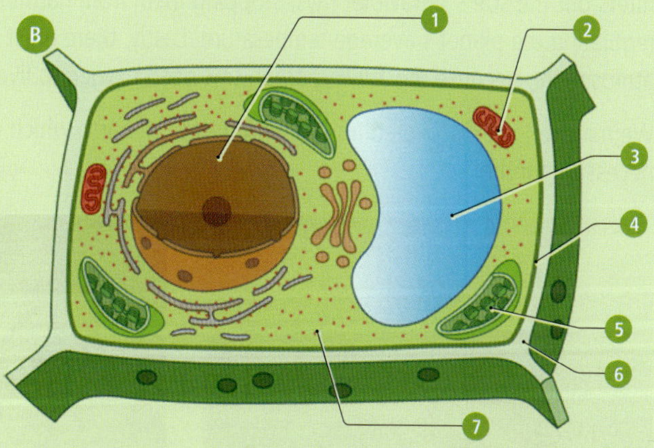

a. Explain the function of each structure or organelle.

b. Give an example of an organism where each type of cell can be found.

22 Read the following text.

> “Your cells are a country of 10 000 trillion citizens, each devoted in some intensively specific way to your overall well-being. There isn't a thing they don't do for you.”
>
> Bill Bryson
> *A Short History of Nearly Everything*
> Transworld Publishers

a. What are the 'country' and the 'citizens' in this text?

b. Is the writer referring to a single-celled organism or a multicellular organism?

c. What are the functions that a cell performs?

Read and think

CAN LIFE EXIST ON OTHER PLANETS?

The existence of life on other planets has been a question without a concrete answer for a long time. This is because life has not yet been discovered outside Earth.

Some scientists believe that some form of extraterrestrial life may exist in places where conditions are suitable. However, it is generally believed that life on these planets would exist only in basic forms, similar to bacteria.

According to a NASA study, one out of every two stars in the Milky Way has planets, but only one out of every two hundred stars has planets in a habitable area. According to this data, of the 50 000 million planets in our galaxy, approximately 500 million planets are in areas where there could be life.

These planets are located in areas with climate and temperature conditions very similar to those on Earth. This means that they meet the conditions necessary for the existence of life. However, an optimal distance from a star that provides light and heat is not the only factor which allows life to develop. The presence of liquid water is also required. Water is an essential component of living organisms and the environment in which many of these organisms live.

It is also necessary for the planet to have a protective atmosphere. The atmosphere filters out the star's ultraviolet rays, stopping them from harming living beings and regulating the planet's average temperature. Lastly, there must be oxygen in the planet's atmosphere, because most living organisms need oxygen to live.

We have not yet discovered any planet apart from Earth which meets all the conditions necessary for life.

The Milky Way galaxy

Earth's hydrosphere

Earth's atmosphere

ANSWER THE QUESTIONS

1. Do all scientists believe that it is possible to find life on other planets?
2. What are the factors that make life on Earth possible?
3. How many planets in the Solar System are in an area with climate and temperature conditions which could permit life?
4. Can we say that there is life on those planets? Why or why not?
5. Have we discovered a planet with the necessary conditions to make life possible?
6. Why do you think many space missions look for liquid water on other planets?

Work it out

CONCEPT MAP

Use the words in the word cloud to create your own unit map in your notebook. Write any connecting texts you need.

class **cells** Fungus prokaryotic Animal order

seven taxa

animal cells plant cells

interaction genus family biomolecules

Monera **Living things**

nutrition reproduction

phylum Plant **five kingdoms** kingdom

vital functions **bioelements**

species eukaryotic Protoctista

SELF-ASSESSMENT

Carry out a self-assessment of what you learned in this unit. Choose one answer for each question and then check your answers.

1. Which of the following factors is not essential for life on Earth?
   - a. Presence of liquid water
   - b. High and low tides
   - c. Optimal distance from the Sun
2. Non-living things ...
   - a. are composed of organic matter.
   - b. do not perform vital functions.
   - c. are composed of bioelements.
3. Autotrophs ...
   - a. transform inorganic substances into organic ones.
   - b. don't need energy from the environment.
   - c. transform organic substances into inorganic ones.

4. The function that enables living organisms to take in matter in order to grow and restore damaged structures and obtain energy is called ...
   - a. nutrition.
   - b. interaction.
   - c. reproduction.
5. Interaction ...
   - a. enables an organism to adapt to external and internal conditions.
   - b. only occurs in animals.
   - c. is not essential to maintain life.
6. Prokaryotic cells ...
   - a. have a defined nucleus.
   - b. do not have a cell membrane.
   - c. are characteristic of bacteria.
7. Plant cells do not have ...
   - a. chloroplasts.
   - b. a centrosome.
   - c. a cell wall.
8. Algae ...
   - a. are autotrophic protoctists.
   - b. are heterotrophic protoctists.
   - c. are prokaryotes.
9. Bacteria ...
   - a. are multicellular organisms.
   - b. are prokaryotic single-celled organisms.
   - c. are eukaryotic single-celled organisms.
10. The science of classifying organisms using a hierarchical system is called ...
    - a. taxonomy.
    - b. taxidermy.
    - c. biology.

02 The simplest life forms

<< LOOKING BACK

- Which kingdoms do the organisms in the images below belong to?
- What type of cell does each organism have?
- What type of nutrition does each organism have?
- Which images show single-celled organisms?
- Which of these organisms are related to images A, B and C?

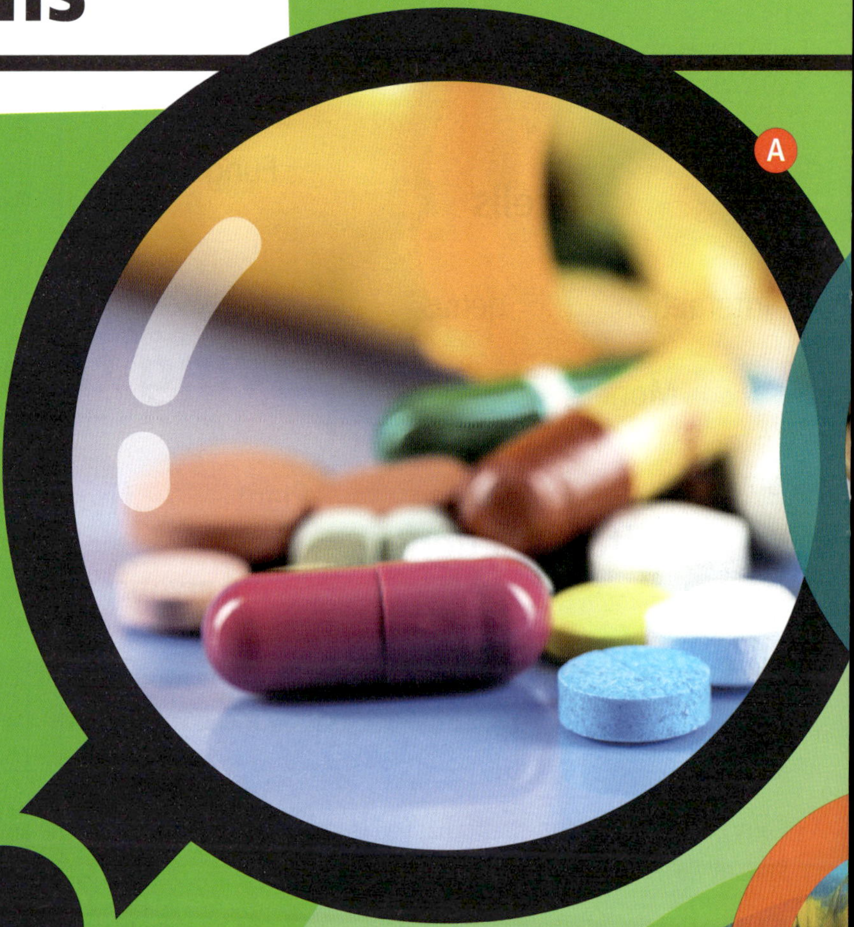

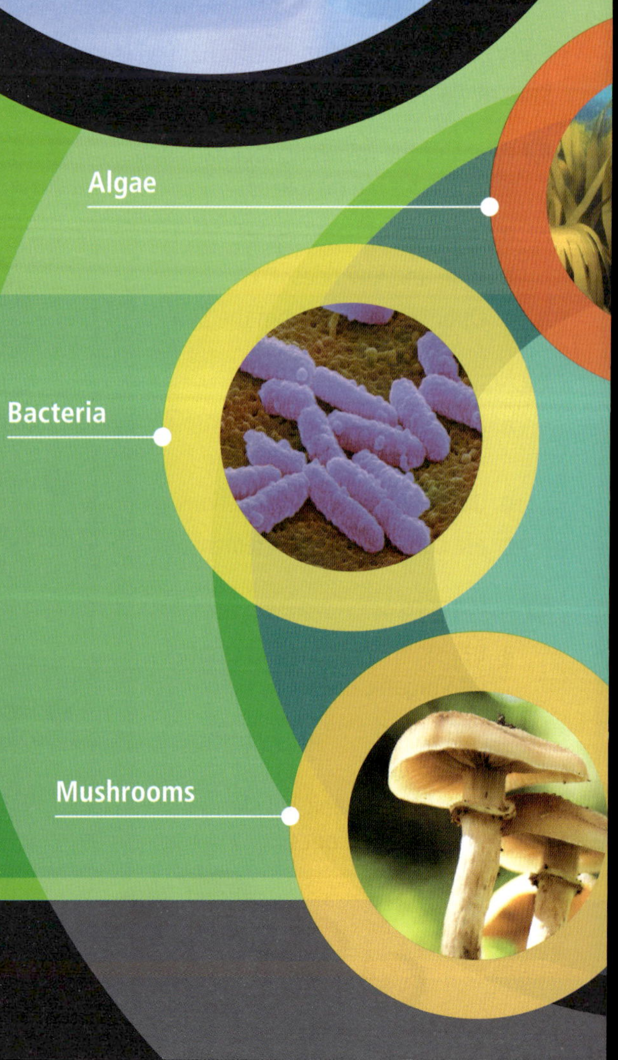

Scientists or detectives?

Scientists are a lot like detectives, searching for a clue to catch a criminal – the key that will unlock a great mystery. The detective has to be careful and observant, looking for anything out of the ordinary, but finding the clue is just the start! Detectives must investigate until they can explain what happened, how it happened, who did it and why. For scientists, it's exactly the same.

One day in 1928, a scientist noticed something strange in his laboratory. He had been working for years on a great mystery. His enemies were so small they couldn't even be seen, but they had killed millions of people all throughout history. The scientist saw that something was growing in his experiment – but instead of destroying his work, it defeated his enemy and would save millions of people in the future.

His discovery may have saved your life. Well done, detective!

?

- Who was the scientist?
- What were the 'enemies'?
- What was growing in the experiment?
- What discovery is the text about?
- What other scientific discoveries that you know have been accidental?

B

C

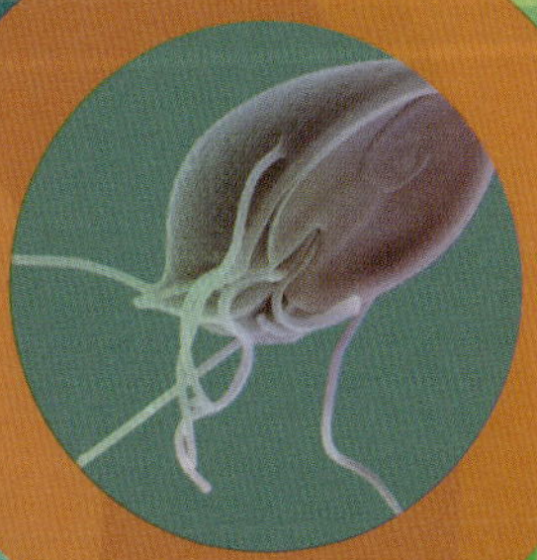

Protozoan

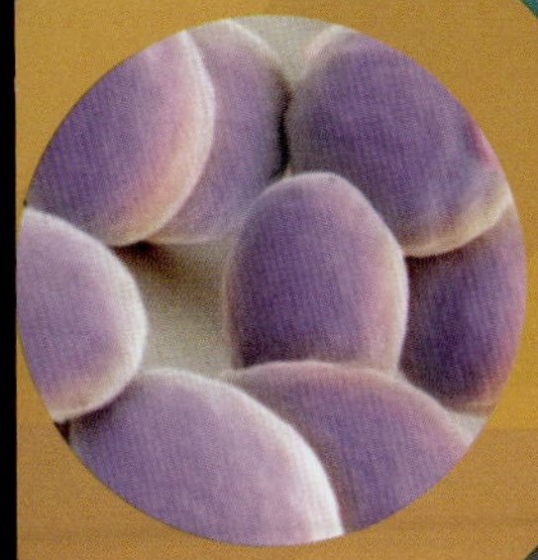

Yeasts

LOOKING FORWARD >>

- Are all bacteria harmful?
- Are all algae visible to the naked eye?
- What is the role of fungi in the environment?
- Can viruses reproduce by themselves?
- What organisms can be found in a puddle?

1 Monerans

Are all bacteria harmful?

The Monera Kingdom consists of all **bacteria**. These are single-celled prokaryotic organisms.

Their **genetic material** (DNA) is not surrounded by a membrane, but dispersed in the cytoplasm. They have a protective **cell wall** around the **cell membrane**.

Bacteria can exist almost anywhere on Earth: in the air, on the land, in the water or inside other living things. Organisms similar to bacteria were the first living things that appeared on Earth.

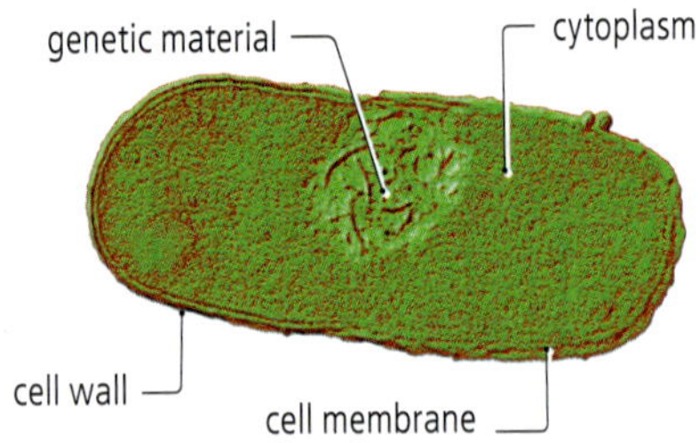

Structure of a bacterium

VITAL FUNCTIONS OF BACTERIA

Nutrition. Bacteria can be **autotrophic** or **heterotrophic**. **Autotrophic** bacteria perform photosynthesis and other different chemical processes to make their own food. **Cyanobacteria** include the photosynthetic bacteria.

Most bacteria are **heterotrophic** and perform the function of nutrition in different ways:

- **Saprotrophic** bacteria feed on dead or **decaying** organisms.
- **Symbiotic** bacteria establish a relationship with other organisms from which both organisms benefit.
- **Parasitic** bacteria live on or in other organisms (hosts). The bacteria benefit but the hosts are damaged.

Reproduction. Bacteria reproduce **asexually** through a process called **binary fission**. This means that a single cell divides into two identical cells. It takes just 20–40 minutes for a bacterium to divide in two.

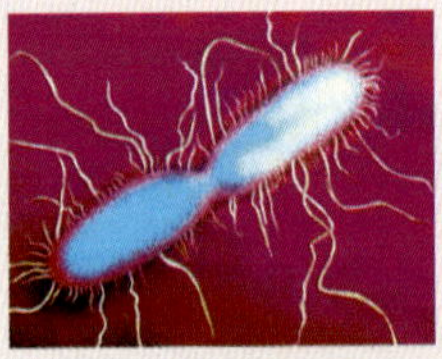

Binary fission

Interaction. Some bacteria have the ability to move using their **flagella** but others cannot move on their own.

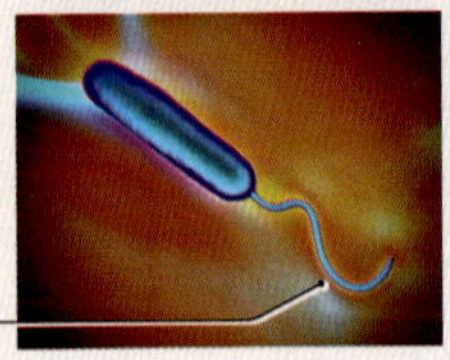

CLASSIFYING BACTERIA

Bacteria can be classified into four groups according to their shape.

Cocci

Bacilli

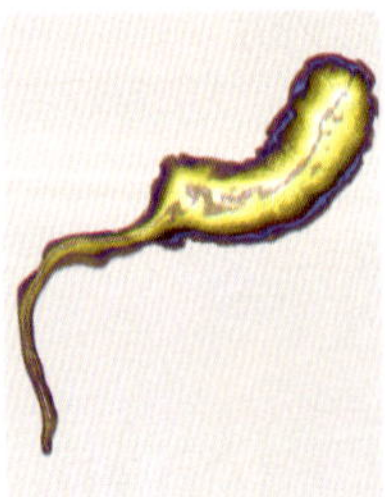

Vibrios

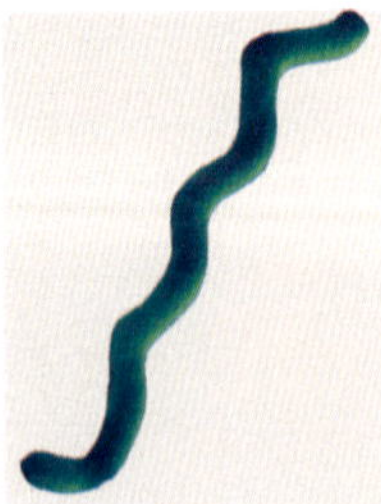

Spirilli

ACTIVITIES

1. Make a drawing of a prokaryotic cell and label its parts.
   a. Why are monerans considered to be prokaryotic organisms?
   b. What are the main differences between prokaryotic cells and eukaryotic cells?
2. Classify bacteria according to their mode of nutrition and their shape.

IMPORTANCE OF BACTERIA

- **In ecosystems.** Bacteria play important roles in ecosystems. Photosynthetic bacteria are **producers** that release oxygen into the atmosphere. Saprotrophic bacteria act as **decomposers** at the end of food chains and food webs. They transform organic matter into inorganic matter.

Colony of **photosynthetic** cyanobacteria

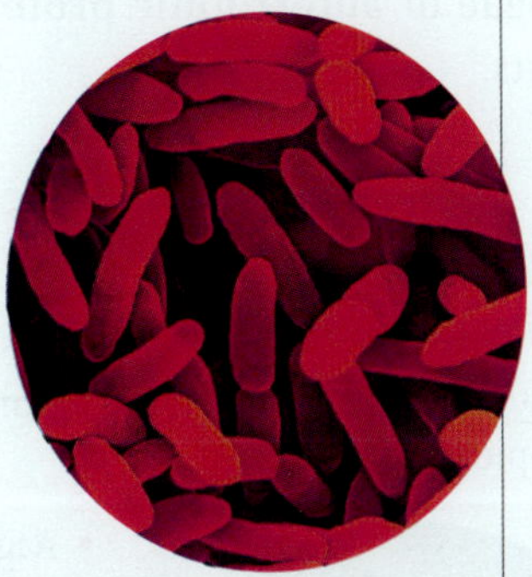

Pseudomonas fluorescens is a **saprophyte**.

- **In food production.** Bacteria are used to make a wide range of food products.

Lactobacillus species (lactic bacteria) are used to produce dairy products such as cheese and yoghurt.

- **In the pharmaceutical industry.** Bacteria are used to produce **antibiotics** and **vaccines** against infectious diseases.
- **Harmful bacteria.** Most bacteria are **beneficial**. Just a few bacteria are **harmful** and cause diseases, such as ear and respiratory diseases, meningitis, pneumonia, tuberculosis, salmonellosis or tetanus. Most bacterial diseases can be treated using **antibiotics**.

Salmonella is a **parasitic bacterium** that infects the human intestines. It is spread by eating contaminated foods, such as eggs, mayonnaise, **poultry** or milk.

BIG THINKER

Alexander Fleming discovered penicillin, a substance that transformed human life. Like vaccination, it was one of the great breakthroughs in the battle against disease and has saved the lives of millions of people. You might think Alexander Fleming was pretty excited when he first saw that a strange mould had killed the bacteria on which he was experimenting, but he just said: *'That's funny'*. Not everyone is so quiet about their brilliant discoveries, though. Do you know who made the most famous exclamation of success in science, and why?

FRIENDLY BACTERIA

Believe it or not, we have more bacteria living in our digestive **passageway** than cells in our entire body. The friendly bacteria that make up our **intestinal flora** help us digest food, destroy pathogens and produce vitamins and natural antibiotics.

ACTIVITIES

3. Are all bacteria harmful? Explain your answer and give examples to support your explanation.
4. Cyanobacteria were formerly called 'blue-green' algae. Do you think this name is correct? Justify your answer.
5. Look for information and find out what *probiotic foods* are. What are their benefits for health?

2 Protoctists

➲ Are all algae visible to the naked eye?

The Protoctista Kingdom includes a diverse group of eukaryotic organisms with no specific tissue structure. They can be single-celled or multicellular.

There are two groups of protoctists: **algae** or **autotrophic protoctists**, and **protozoans** or **heterotrophic protoctists**.

2.1 Algae

Algae are aquatic eukaryotic autotrophic organisms that perform photosynthesis. They appear in various shapes and sizes ranging in size from microscopic algae to giant seaweeds.

- Algae can be **single-celled** or **multicellular**. In some species of unicellular algae, single cells join together to form **colonies**.

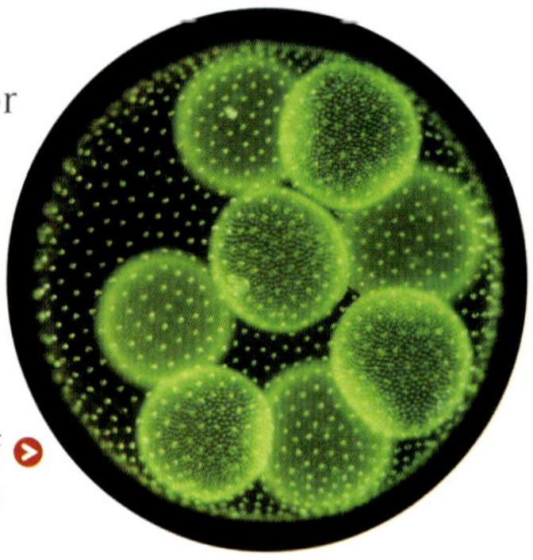

Colony of photosynthetic algae

- Like plants, most algae cells have a cell wall. Algae cells don't form tissue or organs.
- Algae don't have true stems, leaves or roots.
- Algae live in both **fresh** and **seawater aquatic environments** and moist soil habitats. Some spend their life floating (**planktonic**) while others remain attached to the bottom (**benthic**).

VITAL FUNCTIONS OF ALGAE

Nutrition. All algae are autotrophic organisms. In order to perform photosynthesis, algae have **chlorophyll**, which is green, and other **pigments** of different colours, ranging from red to brown.

Reproduction. Algae can reproduce **sexually** (involving male and female gametes), **asexually**, or both ways. Algae reproduce asexually through **binary fission**, **spores** or **fragmentation**. In fragmentation, the body breaks into several fragments and each one develops into an individual algae.

Interaction. Some single-celled algae move using flagella, whereas multicellular algae can't move on their own. Some planktonic algae produce light by **bioluminescence**.

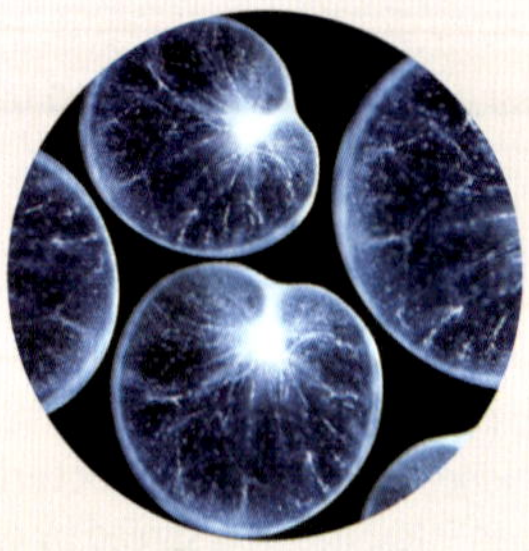

Unicellular algae *Noctiluca* glow in the dark to scare away their predators.

ACTIVITIES

6. Algae perform photosynthesis; does this mean they are plants? Justify your answer. Make a list of the similarities and differences between algae and plants.
7. Explain if the following statement is true or false.

   The criterion used to classify protoctists is the type of reproduction they perform.
8. Some algae are planktonic. Find out what plankton is and what type of organisms make it up. Are they autotrophic or heterotrophic organisms?

CLASSIFYING ALGAE

Green algae are green because of green pigments, mainly chlorophyll. They live in all types of aquatic environment. Green algae store **starch**, a reserve substance also found in plants.

Ulva lactuca also called 'sea lettuce'

Brown algae are brown because of brownish-green pigments. Most are multicellular and grow in marine habitats. Brown algae include **kelp**, the largest protoctists.

Laminaria hyperborea

Red algae have reddish pigments which allow them to perform photosynthesis in much deeper water than green or brown algae. Red algae have been found living in depths of up to 100 m.

Scinaia turgida

IMPORTANCE OF ALGAE

- **In ecosystems.** Algae are the most common **producers** in aquatic ecosystems. They start aquatic food chains, feed aquatic herbivores and produce oxygen that is returned to the atmosphere.
- **In food production and industry.** **Green algae** are a source of **carotene**, which is often used as a food colouring. **Red algae** contain **agar**, a jelly-like substance used as a **thickener** in food, and to prepare **culture dishes** to grow microorganisms. Other red algae contain **carrageenan** used for gelatine capsules and in some cheeses. Certain species of algae are edible and used as **food** because they are rich in vitamins, fibre and proteins.

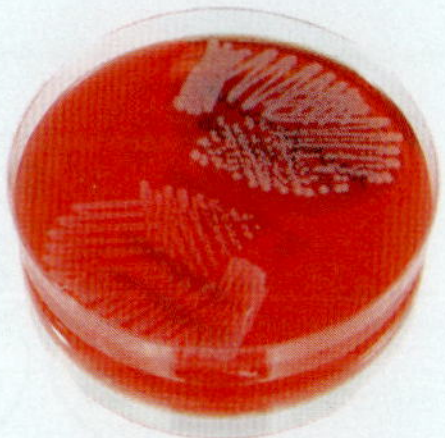

Culture dish

- **Harmful algae.** Certain types of planktonic algae, such as *Noctiluca scintillans*, produce harmful **red tides** when they reproduce excessively. Red tides release potent natural toxins that threaten wildlife, human health, aquatic ecosystems and **fisheries**.

Diatoms are single-celled planktonic algae encased in a silica shell. This is formed by two parts that fit together. They are primary producers that play a key role in aquatic food webs.

ACTIVITIES

9. Which criteria are used to classify algae? Make a table with the different types of algae and their main characteristics.
10. Find out about the uses and benefits of edible seaweeds. In which countries are they usually consumed as a part of the diet?
11. Look for information about the Sargasso Sea. Write a short report on it including its location and the type of algae found there. Why do you think it is usually known as the 'floating desert'?

2.2 Protozoans

Protozoans are single-celled, eukaryotic, heterotrophic organisms. Some protozoans are **free-living** and live in the soil, as well as in fresh or salt water, while others are **parasites.**

Protozoan cells do not have a cell wall and never form tissues.

VITAL FUNCTIONS OF PROTOZOANS

Nutrition. All protozoans are **heterotrophs** and eat bacteria, algae or other protozoans to obtain the nutrients they need to live. Protozoans ingest their food by a process called **phagocytosis**, in which a portion of the cell membrane surrounds a food particle or microorganism, **engulfs** it and brings it into the cell inside a vacuole.

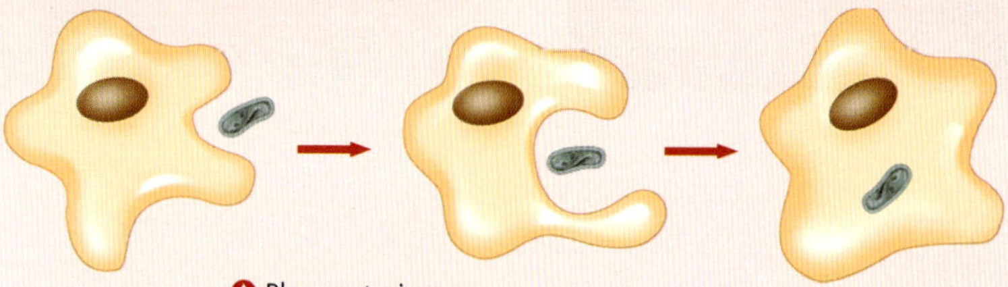

Phagocytosis

Reproduction. Most protozoans reproduce **asexually** either by **binary fission** or **multiple fission**. Some protozoans reproduce sexually, while others use a combination of sexual and asexual reproduction.

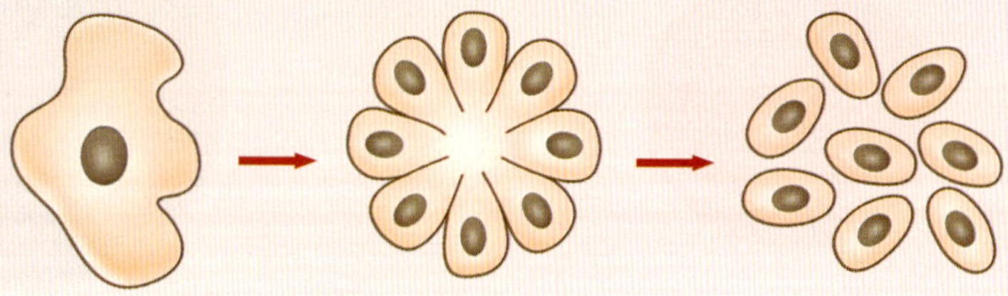

Multiple fission happens when the mother cell divides into multiple daughter cells.

Interaction. Some protozoans are immobile while others move using **cilia, flagella** or **pseudopods** (**false feet**). Pseudopods are projections of the cell cytoplasm.

IMPORTANCE OF PROTOZOANS

- **In ecosystems.** Free-living protozoans are important components of aquatic and soil ecosystems as **primary** or **secondary consumers**. They control the population of soil bacteria by feeding on them. Protozoans also increase soil fertility which intensifies plant growth.
- Protozoans perform several beneficial roles in **wastewater treatment** processes. They break down organic waste substances in the water.
- The skeletal deposits of some dead marine protozoans become fossilised and were converted into important **sedimentary rocks**.
- **Harmful protozoans.** Some protozoans are harmless. However, others can cause serious diseases, such as **sleeping sickness**, **amoebic dysentery**, **malaria** and **Chagas' disease**.

DID YOU KNOW?

Around 130 million years ago, parasitic protozoans called *Plasmodium* evolved. They are transmitted through insect bites and infect animals' blood, making animals sick and transmitting more *Plasmodium* to other animals. Nowadays there are more than 100 species of *Plasmodium*, but just ten cause malaria in humans. Malaria kills hundreds of thousands of people every year, that's why *Plasmodium* is considered to be one of the world's deadliest pathogens.

Where does malaria occur most in the world?

ACTIVITIES

12. Explain the differences between a free-living organism and a parasite. Are protozoans free-living or parasitic?

13. Explain the vital functions of protozoans. Compare these vital functions with those of algae. Make a table to show the similarities and differences.

CLASSIFYING PROTOZOANS

Protozoans are classified into four groups according to the way they move: **flagellates**, **ciliates**, **rhizopods** and **sporozoa**.

Flagellates move using **flagella**. Some are free-living and some are parasites that live in humans and other animals.

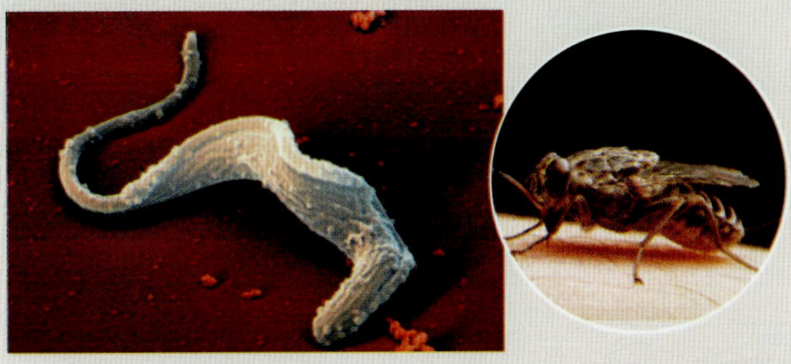

Trypanosoma brucei is a parasite that causes sleeping sickness. It is transmitted by the bite of the tsetse fly.

Ciliates have **cilia** at some point in their life cycle. They can be parasites or free-living. There are also symbiotic ciliates that live in the stomachs of ruminant animals, such as cows, and help them to digest the cellulose of the plants.

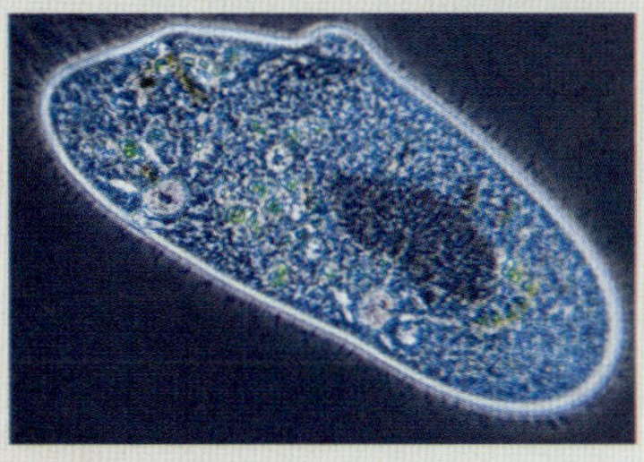

Paramecium also known as 'lady slippers

Rhizopods move using **pseudopods**. These include **amoebas** and **foraminifera**.

Amoebas don't have a shell. They are usually free-living, but also include parasites.

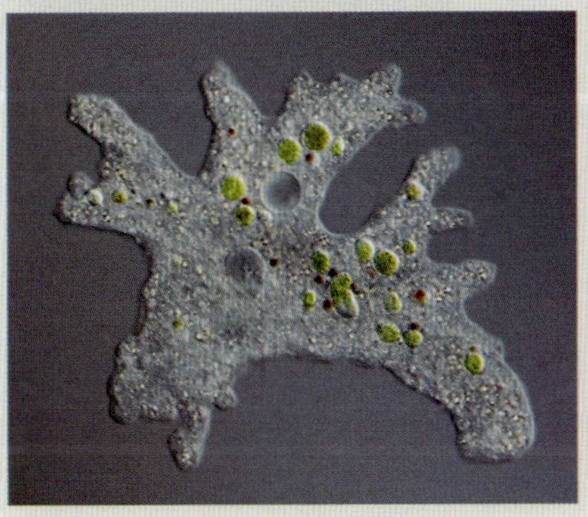

Amoebas move by continually changing the shape of their body, forming pseudopods.

Foraminifera are marine organisms with a calcium carbonate shell.

The accumulation of foraminifera skeletons makes up much of the limestone in the Earth.

Sporozoans are parasitic and immobile. *Plasmodium falciparum* causes malaria, which is transmitted by the bite of the *Anopheles* mosquito.

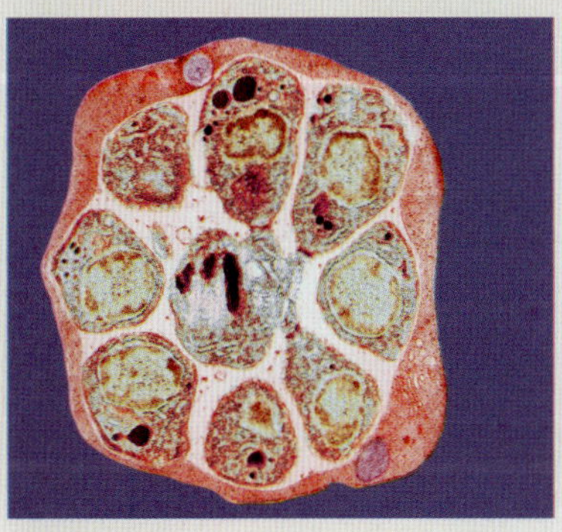

Multiple fission in *Plasmodium falciparum*.

ACTIVITIES

14. Explain the criterion used to classify protozoans. Compare it with the criterion used to classify algae; are the criteria the same?

15. Give examples of harmful and beneficial protozoans. Explain your answers.

16. Search for information on the Internet about the following human diseases and complete the table below in your notebook.

	microorganism responsible	way of transmission	symptoms	countries affected
sleeping sickness				
malaria				
amoebic dysentery				
Chagas' disease				

3 Fungi

What is the role of fungi in the environment?

The Fungus Kingdom includes eukaryotic, heterotrophic organisms.

- Fungi cells have a cell wall similar to that of plants, but it doesn't contain cellulose. They don't have chloroplasts and don't form tissues.
- Fungi grow in the soil, in dark, damp places or on the organic matter they feed on.
- They can be **single-celled**, such as **yeasts**, or **multicellular**, such as **moulds** and **mushrooms**.

STRUCTURE OF A MUSHROOM

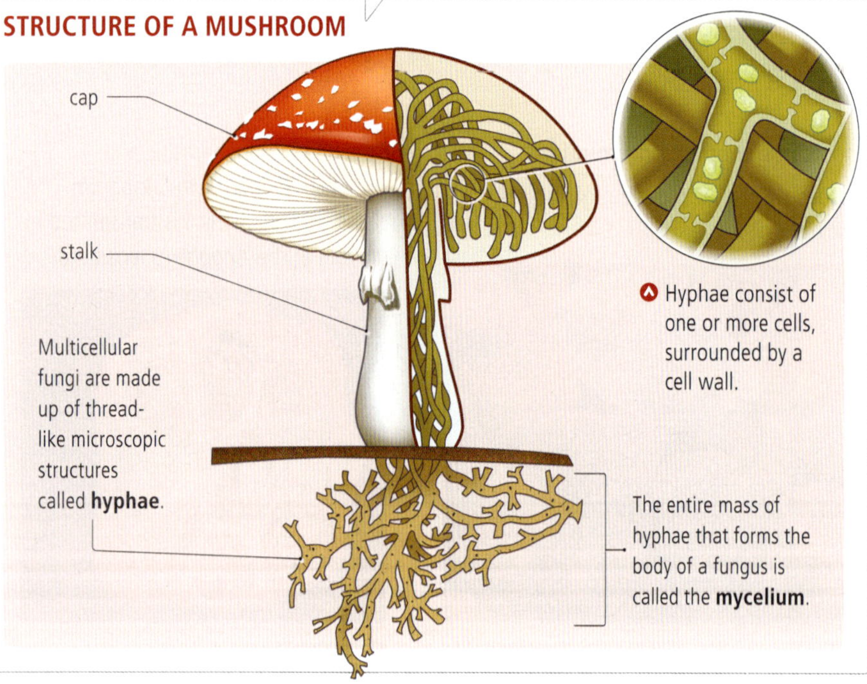

DID YOU KNOW?

Have you ever heard the expression *'to be worth its weight in gold'*? Gold is valued at about 35 euros per gram, but some fungi are worth much more. In 2007, a white truffle weighing 1.5 kg was bought for about 300 000 euros. That's 200 euros per gram! You might have 8 or 9 g of truffles on pasta – a very expensive meal!

What other expensive foods are there?

Truffles

VITAL FUNCTIONS OF FUNGI

Nutrition. All fungi are **heterotrophic**. They get the nutrients they need in different ways.

- **Saprophytic fungi** feed on decomposing organic matter from other living things. Most fungi belong to this group.
- **Parasitic fungi** cause diseases in plants and animals.
- **Symbiotic fungi** establish **symbiotic** relationships with other organisms. **Lichens** are organisms formed by a symbiotic relationship between a **fungus** and an **alga**. Both organisms contribute to and benefit from this relationship. The fungus provides moisture and mineral salts. The alga provides food produced through photosynthesis.

Lichen on a tree

Reproduction. Fungi reproduce **asexually** by producing **spores** or **gemmation**. Spores are produced in multicellular mushrooms on special cells located on the underside of the cap. Some fungi reproduce **sexually**.

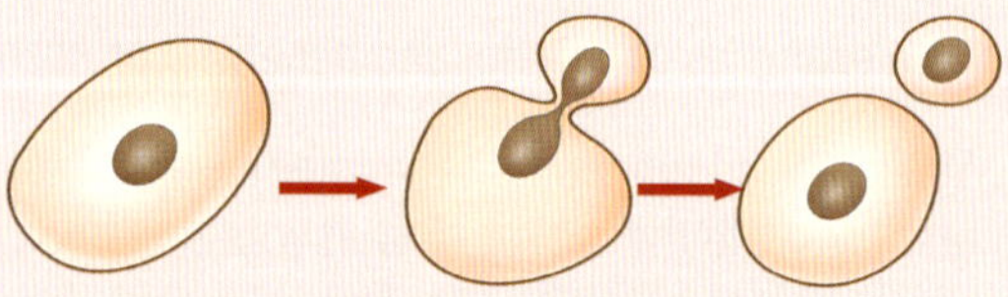

Gemmation in yeasts. The new offspring cell begins as a small outgrowth on the membrane of the parent cell. It remains attached as it grows, separating only when it is mature.

Interaction. Fungi are immobile.

CLASSIFYING FUNGI

UNICELLULAR FUNGI

Yeasts are unicellular fungi. Some yeasts are harmful while others are beneficial.

Candida albicans causes human thrush.

MULTICELLULAR FUNGI

Moulds are multicellular filamentous fungi. They grow on decomposing organic matter, like tree trunks, fruit, cheese and bread.

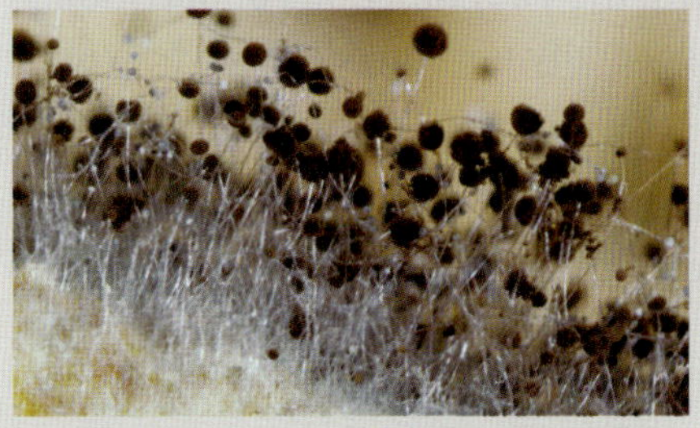

Genus *Rhizopus* (common bread mould)

Mushrooms are multicellular fungi which generally consist of a stalk with a large cap on top.

Amanita phalloides, known as 'death cap mushroom', is poisonous and usually deadly.

IMPORTANCE OF FUNGI

- **In ecosystems.** Fungi are **decomposers** at the end of food chains and food webs. They break down decaying organic matter in the ecosystems and transform it into inorganic matter.
- **In industry and food production.** Many species of mushrooms are edible and delicious, but others are poisonous. Yeasts perform the process of **fermentation** through which they transform sugars into alcohol and carbon dioxide. That's why they are useful in the food industry.

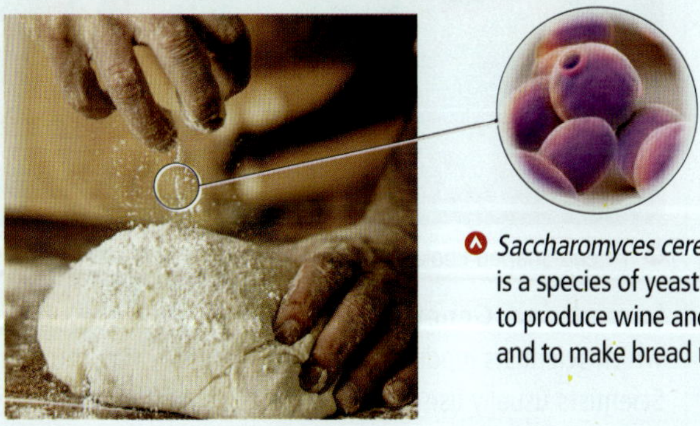

Saccharomyces cerevisiae is a species of yeast used to produce wine and beer and to make bread rise.

- **In medicine.** Yeasts are eukaryotic, like humans. That's why performing experiments on yeast can provide data that can be applied to humans. Many fungi also produce **antibiotic** substances, which are used to treat bacterial diseases.

The antibiotic penicillin is derived from the mould *Penicillium.*

- **Harmful fungi.** Parasitic fungi cause infections in humans called mycosis. Examples of mycosis include **ringworm, athlete's foot** and **thrush**.

ACTIVITIES

17. Lichens are an alliance between kingdoms.
   a. What kingdoms does this sentence refer to?
   b. What is this 'alliance' called?
   c. What are the benefits of this 'alliance'?

18. Classify fungi according to their type of nutrition and number of cells.

19. Mycorrhiza is a symbiotic association between a fungus and the roots of a plant. Search for information about the benefits they obtain.

20. Make a list of the importance and benefits of the three different groups of fungi.

21. Find out what truffles are and what they are used for.

4 What is a virus?

> Can viruses reproduce by themselves?

A virus is a non-cellular parasite that can reproduce only by invading the cells of other living things. Outside a host, viruses are inert. Viruses have no proper cell structure (non-cellular) and don't perform the vital functions of nutrition and interaction. As a consequence, they are generally not considered to be true living things.

Viruses infect cells of all types of organisms: animals, plants, bacteria, fungi, algae and protozoans. Viruses that infect bacteria are called **bacteriophages** or **phages**.

STRUCTURE OF VIRUSES

Viruses consist of a strand of **nucleic acid** (**DNA** or **RNA**) as genetic material, surrounded by a protective protein coat called **capsid**.

Some viruses, such as the influenza virus, have a further **membrane envelope** of lipid, surrounding the protein.

Other viruses also have a **tail**.

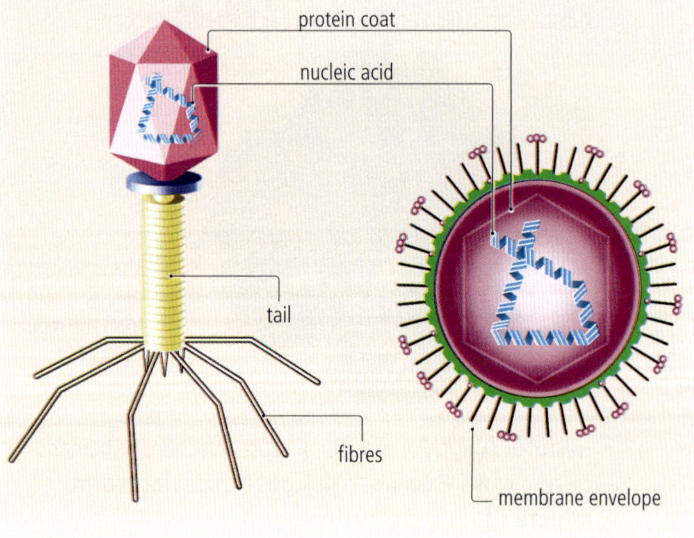

Bacteriophage

Influenza virus

IMPORTANCE OF VIRUSES

Harmful viruses. Examples of common human diseases caused by viruses include the **common cold**, the **flu**, **chickenpox** and **mumps**. Serious diseases such as **Ebola**, **AIDS**, **bird flu** and **swine flu** are all also caused by viruses. Plants also suffer from viral diseases, such as the **tobacco mosaic virus**.

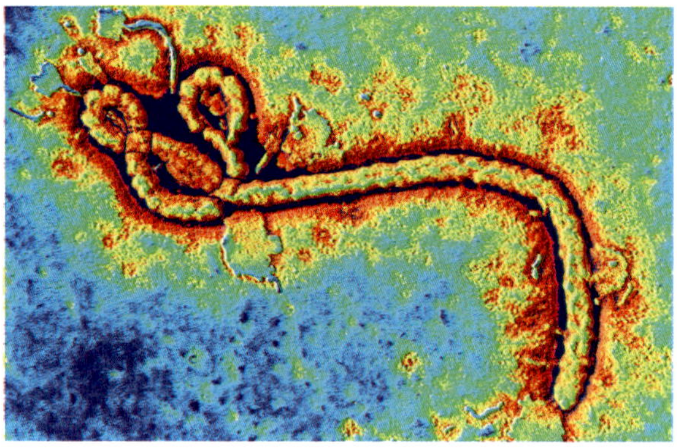

Thread-shaped Ebola virus

In medicine. **Genetic engineering** is the process by which scientists modify the genetic material of an organism. Scientists usually use viruses, such as phages, to introduce the modified genetic material into the host cells. That's the way human insulin is produced for diabetic patients.

ACTIVITIES

22. Do viruses meet all the criteria of the generally accepted definition of life? Which ones do viruses meet and which ones do they fail to meet?

23. Decide whether the sentence below is true or false and explain your answer.

Viruses are often considered non-living as they exist in an inert state outside a host cell.

24. Look for information about the Ebola virus and write a short report about it. You should include information on the following: a description of the virus, its geographic distribution, the incubation period, diagnosis, possible treatment, mortality rates, vaccines and recent outbreaks.

Discovery techniques

What organisms can be found in a puddle?

Life forms in a puddle

A surprising number of microscopic organisms make their homes in puddles and other temporary bodies of water.

ONCE YOU'VE FINISHED, WASH YOUR HANDS THOROUGHLY AND CLEAN ALL THE EQUIPMENT YOU USED.

AIMS

- Find out what organisms live in a puddle.

MATERIALS

- water from a puddle
- a small plastic bottle
- a pipette
- a microscope slide and a slide cover
- a microscope

PROCEDURE

1. Look for a pond, preferably one with a soil bottom and with plants nearby. You might find one in a park, forest or garden. Dip a small plastic bottle into the water and collect a sample. Put the lid on the bottle.
2. Use a pipette to take some water out of the bottle. Squeeze the bulb of the pipette first to expel any air from inside it. Now dip the tip of the pipette in the water. Reduce the pressure of your fingers on the bulb. Water will enter the tube. Fill the pipette halfway.
3. Squeeze the bulb again to put a drop of water on a microscope slide. Cover the droplet with a slide cover. Try not to let any air bubbles form.
4. Look at the droplet using the lowest magnification on the microscope. Draw what you see, noting down the magnification each time (multiply the power of the objective lens by the power of the ocular lens or eyepiece).
5. Repeat the process with the other lenses, increasing the magnification. Draw the microorganisms that you can see.

CONCLUSIONS

1. Based on the appearance of the observed microorganisms say whether they are protozoans, algae or fungi. Can you see any animals or plants? What about bacteria?
2. Look for pictures of the following microorganisms on the Internet: *cyanobacterium, euglena, vorticella, paramecium, amoeba, spirogyra, volvox, cosmarium, cyclops, daphnia* and *rotifer.* Compare them with the microorganisms you drew earlier and try to identify them. If you can't identify them all, look for pictures of more microorganisms.
3. Share your findings with the rest of the class. Which microorganisms appeared most frequently in your samples?

Revision activities

1. Describe the main characteristics of bacteria. What type of cells do bacteria have?

2. Why do you think protozoans are considered the most animal-like organisms? Explain why they are not classified as animals.

3. There is a type of bioluminescent bacteria that lives inside the anglerfish. The light lures prey for the anglerfish in deep-sea waters. Decide how you would characterise the relationship between the anglerfish and the bacteria inside it, and why.

4. Make drawings of the different types of bacteria according to their shape.

5. The Grand Prismatic Spring in Yellowstone National Park (Wyoming, USA) has stunning natural colours that come from bacteria. Read about this unusual spring and write a short report about how the bacteria live in such an extreme environment, and why the spring has so many colours.

6. Many foods can be pasteurised, such as milk and fruit juice. What health benefit are there with pasteurisation?

7. Many foods, such as dairy products, contain helpful bacteria. Search on the Internet for information about how yoghurt is made, and explain why it tastes sour.

8. In what ways are bacteria beneficial to us? Explain where these helpful bacteria live.

9. Explain what could happen to an ecosystem if algae stop thriving.

10. In the nineteenth century, Ireland was devastated by a potato famine. Do some research on the famine and write a short report about the fungus that caused it.

11. What type of organism is a lichen? Do some research and write a short report on it.

12. Complete the table to show the similarities and differences between algae and protozoans.

algae	protozoans	both

13. Say whether the following sentence is true or false, and explain your answer:

    If a microorganism moves with flagella it must be a protozoan.

14. Explain whether you would classify protozoans as harmful or helpful, and why.

15. *Naegleria fowleri* is an amoeba which causes a condition known as primary amoebic meningoencephalitis (PAM) in humans. Do some research on this infection and find out:

    a. where the microorganism is found
    b. how it enters the human body

16. Explain the ways that fungi can reproduce. Then, do a drawing to illustrate one of these methods.

17. Look at the following pictures and say:

    a. the type of fungus shown
    b. if it is a unicellular or a multicellular organism

A

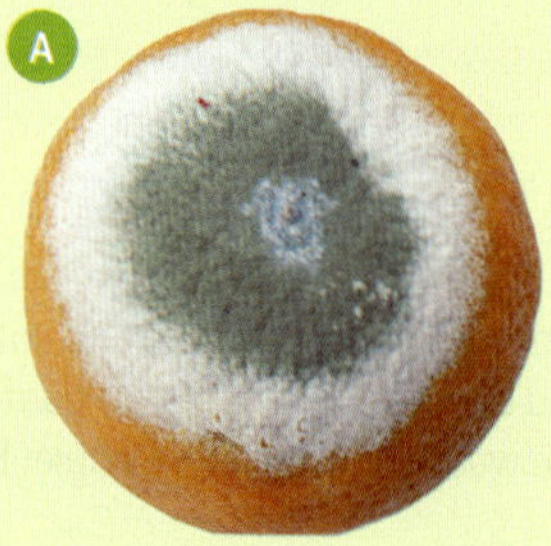

B

18. Decide if the following text is true or false, and explain your answer.

    A brown-coloured organism is discovered growing on a tree trunk. Studies show it is non-photosynthetic and lives off the decaying matter of the tree. These studies conclude that the organism cannot be a fungus.

19. Identify one way that fungi and plants are similar. Then, list two ways that fungi and plants are different.

20. How are fungi beneficial or detrimental to the environment or humans?

21. Penicillin was the first medically useful antibiotic – in fact, it was originally known as the 'wonder drug'. Search on the Internet to explain how penicillin works. Then, explain which type of fungi it comes from.

22. Athlete's foot, or *tinea pedis* is a common skin infection caused by a fungus. Search on the Internet for information about this microorganism and write a short report about it. Make sure to include:

    a. the ideal environment for the fungus
    b. any signs and symptoms of the condition
    c. how to avoid catching athlete's foot

23 Mildew is a harmful fungus that can cause an allergic reaction in humans. It can be found on decaying materials or on the surface of objects. One common place to find mildew is on shower curtains. Think back to what you learned about athlete's foot. What conditions do you think make it likely to find mildew in the bathroom?

24 When preserving food at home it is very important to avoid the bacteria that cause botulism. Research foodborne botulism and complete the sentences:

a. Botulism is caused by …
b. Symptoms of foodborne botulism include …
c. Botulism can be prevented by …
d. When sterilising equipment (for example, jars of food) make sure to heat them to … for … minutes.
e. In addition to food, bacteria for botulism can also be found in …

25 Look at the diagram below. Name and explain the process it shows.

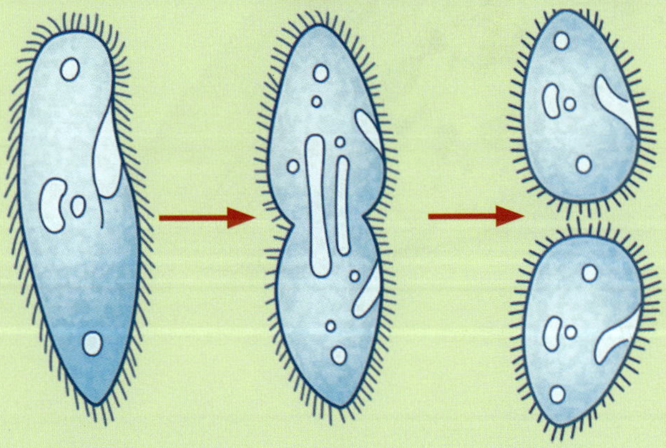

a. What vital function is this process related to?
b. Can you recognise the organism in the diagram? What group of organisms does it belong to?

26 Draw and describe the structure of:

a. a virus that can infect humans
b. a bacteriophage

27 Explain what vital functions viruses don't share with living things.

28 Stromatolites, the oldest known fossils on Earth, were formed by the growth of layer upon layer of cyanobacteria. Use the Internet to find information on where they can be found and what they look like. Write a short report.

29 Viruses, such as Ebola, can spread very quickly. Imagine that a foodborne virus breaks out in your community. With a partner, discuss which of the following practices would be most effective to stop the outbreak. Consider the advantages and disadvantages of each suggestion. You may also add individual ideas.

- vaccinate everyone
- boil drinking water
- wash your hands frequently
- wash food carefully
- stay home if you are sick
- wear a face mask
- do not share cups, glasses, dishes or cutlery
- restrict travel in and out of affected areas
- prohibit the sharing of magazines in a medical waiting room or common area

30 Say whether the following terms are related to bacteria, fungi, protozoa or viruses:

a. cavities (dental caries)
b. staphylococcus
c. salmonella
d. polio
e. lyme disease
f. candidiasis
g. amoebic dysentery
h. the common cold
i. ringworm
j. sleeping sickness

31 Some viruses, such as the influenza virus, can mutate.

a. How does this help the virus survive?
b. Does it have anything to do with the fact that we need to get a new flu vaccine each year?

32 The smallpox virus has had a considerable impact around the world. It has also been around for a long time. It is believed that Pharaoh Ramses V died from smallpox! Search for information about smallpox. In your notebook, copy and complete the timeline of major events in the 'life' of the virus. Finally, explain what kind of threat smallpox presents now.

33 Decide whether the sentence below is true or false and explain your answer.

Malaria is a harmful virus spread by mosquitoes.

34 Brazilian researchers have been using mosquitoes to fight the virus that causes dengue fever. Search for information and explain how genetic engineering is helping researchers fight this virus.

Read and Think

HARNESSING HELPFUL MICROORGANISMS

Although some microorganisms cause health problems, they are much more our friends than our enemies. In fact, many everyday foods contain these helpful bacteria and fungi! These tiny organisms change the sugars and proteins in foods into new products with different flavours. Bread, cheese, yoghurt, beer and wine are all products of this transformation.

For example, cheeses can be **inoculated** with a fungus. Fungi produce digestive enzymes which break down protein molecules. Mould growing on Camembert cheese breaks down the product, making the centre very soft.

Bacteria are also an essential ingredient for making yoghurt. After milk is boiled, bacteria are added to convert the lactose (sugar) in the milk into acid. This reaction causes the milk to become thick because the acid **curdles** the milk. Yoghurt is a food that contains probiotics, good bacteria that are helpful for our digestive tract. Foods made with microorganism are also thought to be more digestible because sugars and proteins are partially broken down.

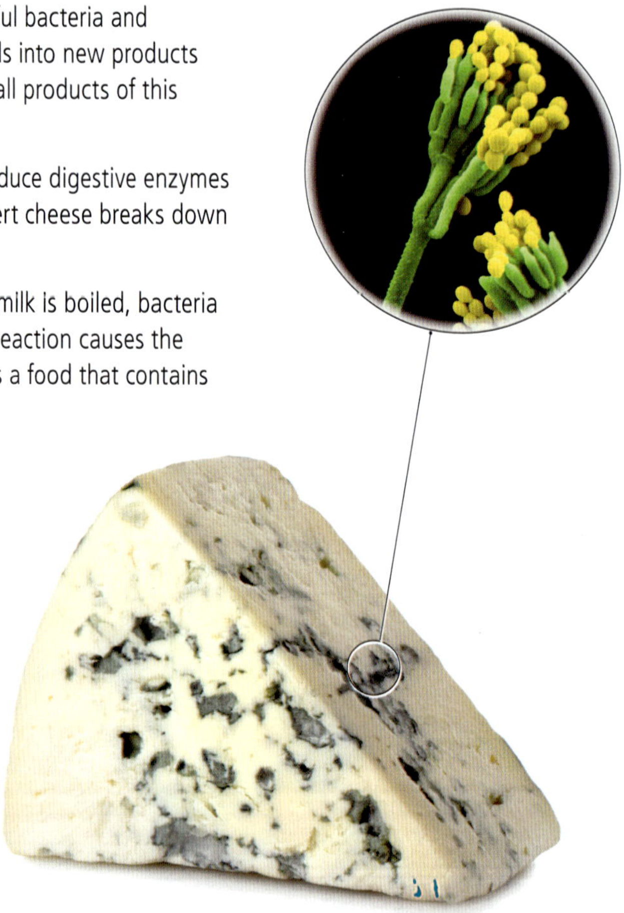

Food isn't the only thing to benefit from bacteria and fungi; biotechnology researchers are also **harnessing** the benefits of microorganisms. Scientists now use bacteria in the production of antibiotics, enzymes and **steroids**. These modified microorganisms, known as transgenic bacteria, are found in some medications. There are even transgenic goats whose milk is beneficial for stopping **blood clots**! To achieve this, scientists inject the modified DNA sequence into goat ova and insert them into goats. Scientists then extract a drug from the offspring's milk. This drug is later used to prevent blood clots during surgery!

ANSWER THE QUESTIONS

1. Write down the foods you eat in a week that contain beneficial bacteria, fungi or yeast. After making the list, ask your partner the following questions:
   a. How often do you eat beneficial microorganisms?
   b. Do these foods contain yeast, fungi or bacteria?
2. How did humans first learn to make cheese? Search for information and write a short report on the subject.
3. Decide whether *Penicillium camemberti* and *Penicillium roqueforti* are bacteria or fungi. Where do their names come from?
4. Explain why the taste of camembert cheese is often compared to mushrooms.
5. **Buttermilk** is used for baking bread in several countries. Companies make it by inoculating milk with the *Lactobacillus* bacteria. If you cannot find buttermilk in a shop, you can easily create a substitute at home by adding one tablespoon of lemon juice or vinegar to one cup of milk. Why do you think this makes a good substitute for buttermilk?
6. Explain why vegans or strict vegetarians may want to avoid transgenic bacteria.
7. Genetically modified bacteria are being used in healthcare. They can be used to produce insulin, the hepatitis B vaccine and human growth hormones. Look up information about genetically modified bacteria in medicine and write about one of its applications.

Work it out

CONCEPT MAP

Use the words in the word cloud to create your own unit map in your notebook. Write any connecting texts you need.

Monerans cocci algae brown algae **Fungi** mushrooms

vibrios rhizopods spirilli red algae bacilli diatoms

flagellates **The simplest Kingdoms** moulds

green algae protozoans

ciliates bacteria **Protoctists** yeasts sporozoans

SELF-ASSESSMENT

Carry out a self-assessment of what you learned in this unit. Choose one answer for each question and then check your answers.

1. Bacteria are …
   a. prokaryotic organisms.
   b. eukaryotic organisms.
   c. both procaryotic and eukaryotic.

2. Bacteria are important because …
   a. they are used in antibiotic production.
   b. some of them are decomposers.
   c. both a and b

3. Multicellular algae …
   a. are heterotrophic protoctists.
   b. always have green pigments to perform photosynthesis.
   c. belong to the kingdom protoctists.

4. Autotrophic protoctists are …
   a. unicellular and multicellular algae.
   b. parasites.
   c. algae and some free-living protozoans.

5. What role do protozoans have in an ecosystem?
   a. They are producers.
   b. They are decomposers.
   c. They are primary or secondary consumers.

6. Protozoans are classified according to …
   a. their shape.
   b. the way they move.
   c. the number of cilia they have.

7. Protozoans reproduce …
   a. sexually by pseudopods.
   b. asexually by binary or multiple fission.
   c. both a and b

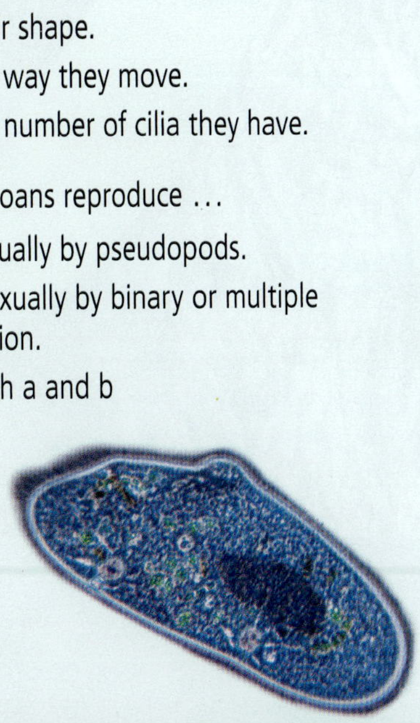

8. Gemmation is a type of …
   a. sexual reproduction.
   b. asexual reproduction typical of yeasts.
   c. asexual reproduction common in algae.

9. Fungi …
   a. can be parasitic, saprophytic or symbiotic.
   b. are made of thread-like structures called hyphae.
   c. feed on primary and secondary consumers.

10. Viruses are parasites that …
   a. reproduce asexually.
   b. reproduce sexually.
   c. reproduce by invading the cells of living organisms.

03 Plants

<< LOOKING BACK

- Look at the photo of the bee. How are insects involved in the plant life cycle?
- What are the three parts that most plants have in common? Which part is not shown in the pictures below?
- Plants cannot move, but they can interact with their environment. Think of as many examples of plant interactions as you can.
- Do gymnosperms have leaves? Describe them.
- The corn growing in the photo below will be consumed by human beings. Where do plants get their food from?

Strange movements

There are some strange and beautiful plants in the natural world – some of them even move. One, originally from a region near Washington in North America, has two pink and green leaves with long, thin spikes like fingers at their edges. There are little hairs on the surface of the leaves, and if you touch them the two leaves close like a book!

In South Africa there is another moving plant called the Cape Sundew. It gets part of its name from the Cape of Good Hope where it grows in the wild. The other part of its name comes from shining beads of glue on its leaves, which are covered in little red tentacles. If anything touches the gluey tentacles, the leaf slowly curls up, covering it in more and more of the glue.

?

- Why do you think plants would behave this way?

LOOKING FORWARD >>

- What are thylakoids?
- How do non-flowering plants reproduce?
- What are the names of the two types of plant stem? How are they different?
- What is phloem sap?
- How are plants able to move?
- Why do flowering plants grow fruit?
- Why do plants become endangered? Can you think of some endangered species of plant?
- Which gas do plants give off at night?
- How can we accurately identify different types of trees?

1 Plants

What are thylakoids?

The Plant Kingdom includes over 300 000 species including trees, mosses, ferns and cacti, amongst many others. Most plants produce seeds.

All plants have two things in common:

- They use the light from the Sun to make energy.
- They adapt to their environment.

Plants are **eukaryotes:** In their cells the nucleus is separate from the cytoplasm.

They are all **multicellular** organisms: they are made up of many cells that form groups to carry out specific functions.

Plants are **autotrophs:** they produce their own food by carrying out photosynthesis. To do this they need sunlight, water and carbon dioxide.

Many plants contain **vascular tissue**: cells used for transporting water and minerals to different parts of the organism.

Most plants, although not all, have **leaves**, a **stem** and **roots**. The green colour of plants comes from **chlorophyll**. This **pigment** is essential to photosynthesis.

Most plants inhabit the ground, and are fixed into the Earth with roots. However, they may turn **slightly** or open and close their leaves and petals. Some plants have adapted to living in water.

MORE ABOUT CHLOROPHYLL

In eukaryotic plant cells, chlorophyll is contained in **chloroplasts**, the part of the cell where photosynthesis occurs.

Chloroplasts convert energy from the **Sun** into **sugar** that can be used by the plant as food.

Chlorophyll molecules sit on the surface of chloroplast compartments, called **thylakoids**, where the light reactions of photosynthesis take place.

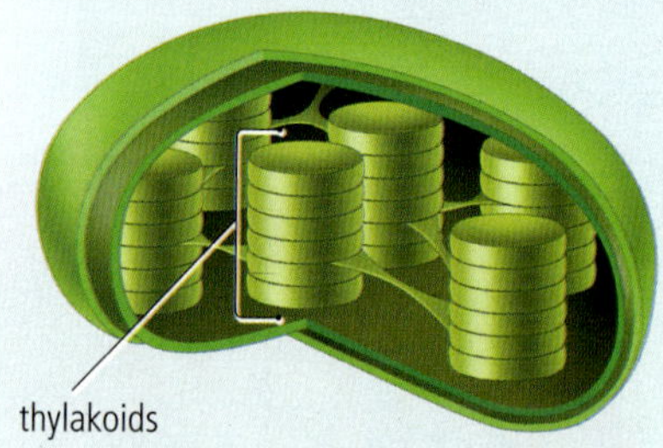

ACTIVITIES

1. Where do most plants live? What are the three parts that most have in common?
2. What is the use of vascular tissue? Is it found in all plants?
3. Plant cells contain chlorophyll. Name the other parts of a plant cell. How do they differ from animal cells and prokaryotic cells?

Classification

Plants can be classified into two main groups.

NON-FLOWERING PLANTS

Non-flowering plants do not have flowers, fruit or seeds. They reproduce by using **spores**. This group includes:

- **Bryophytes:** These plants have no roots, stem or leaves. They don't have vascular tissue.
- **Pteridophytes:** Unlike bryophytes, these plants have vascular tissue.

Liverworts

Moss

Ferns

Horsehair

FLOWERING PLANTS

All flowering plants have flowers and seeds. They contain vascular tissue. This group includes:

- **Angiosperms:** The flowers of these plants produce seeds that **grow inside fruit**. This is the most common group of plants.
- **Gymnosperms:** The seeds produced by these plants **do not grow inside fruit**.

An orange tree is an angiosperm.

Gymnosperm seeds grow inside cones.

BIG THINKER

Anna Atkins had an unusually scientific education for a woman in the 19th century; her greatest interest was botany. Anna was the first woman in the world to publish a book of photographs. She made beautifully detailed pictures of dried plants using an early photographic technique called cyanotype that created blue-coloured images. What other equipment, other than a camera, is useful for studying plants?

ACTIVITIES

4. What is the main difference between gymnosperms and angiosperms?
5. Which type of plant has no vascular tissue?
6. We consume the stem, roots, leaves, fruit and seeds of plants as food. Think of ten edible plants and make a table to show which parts we eat, giving an example of each part. Start with *orange*.

2 Non-flowering plants

How do non-flowering plants reproduce?

Non-flowering plants do not have flowers, seeds or fruit.

- They usually live in moist environments.
- They reproduce by dispersing reproductive cells called **spores**.
- There are various groups of non-flowering plants, including **bryophytes** and **pteridophytes.**

Fern spores with sporangia

2.1 Bryophytes

Bryophytes are small, primitive plants that don't have roots or vascular tissue.

- They are land plants: they need moisture and shade to survive.
- They live on rocks, trees, walls and roofs.
- They don't have vascular tissue, so water and minerals are absorbed by the whole body of the plant through the cuticle layer.
- The largest group of bryophytes is **mosses.** These plants sometimes form a soft carpet in woods and moist gardens.

Moss covering a tree and rocks

MOSSES HAVE THE FOLLOWING STRUCTURE:

OTHER BRYOPHYTE TYPES

Another group of bryophytes is **liverworts**. These plants do not have caulidium or phylidia. They have lobed leaves that connect directly to rhizoids and the earth below.

BRYOPHYTES AND THE ENVIRONMENT

Bryophytes provide excellent erosion protection to soil. They also help other plants to grow and provide food and shelter for animals.

ACTIVITIES

7. Non-flowering plants often live near water. Why is this?
8. How are liverworts different to mosses? Which bryophyte group is more common?
9. Both bryophytes and pteridophytes produce spores. Explain the differences in the way the two groups form their spores.

2.2 Pteridophytes

Pteridophytes are generally larger than bryophytes. They have vascular tissue, roots, a stem and leaves, through which they transport food produced by photosynthesis, as well as water and minerals.

- Like bryophytes, they live on land in moist environments near bodies of water. They need moisture to reproduce.
- The largest group of pteridophytes is **ferns**.

DID YOU KNOW?

350 million years ago the Earth was covered in rainforest. Changes in temperature and the atmosphere meant new kinds of forest took over. This was the Carboniferous period, when ferns and horsetails grew as tall as modern day trees! Over time, those plants were transformed into the coal we now burn as **fuel**. How did this transformation happen?

FERNS HAVE THE FOLLOWING STRUCTURE:

Sorus: a group of sporangia that appears on the back of fern fronds during the reproduction period.

Rhizomes: thick stems that grow underground.

Roots: these fix the plant in the ground and absorb water and minerals. They connect to the rhizomes.

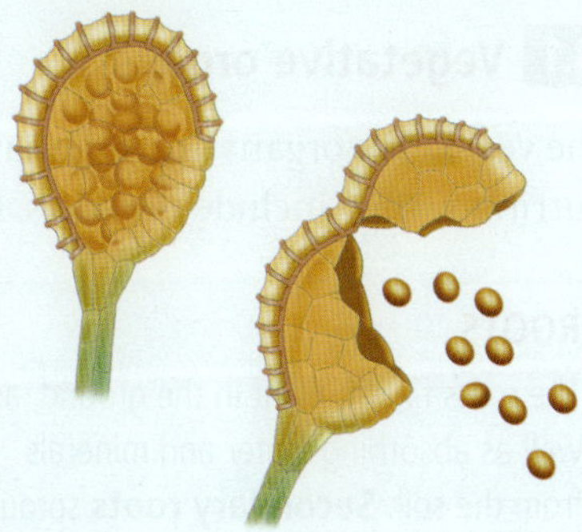

Sporangium: single-cell fern spores grow in the sporangium. When **released** they fall to the ground. If there is enough moisture they germinate and new plants grow.

Fronds: fern leaves that grow from the rhizomes. They are split into different segments

PTERIDOPHYTES AND THE ENVIRONMENT

Ferns are an excellent **indicator species** for testing the health of an ecosystem. For example, they can detect changes in water quality and are excellent indicators of climate change.

OTHER PTERIDOPHYTE TYPES

Other types of pteridophyte include **horsetails** and **club mosses**. Horsetails have non-photosynthetic shoots that come from long, hollow, photosynthetic stems.

Horsetails

ACTIVITIES

10. Describe the functional differences between the underground parts of bryophytes and pteridophyes. Which group do you think is most similar to a flowering plant? Why?

11. Investigate the Carboniferous Period. Write a report on the plant and animal species of the period and describe why it ended.

12. North American Indians used moss as bedding. Why was it suitable for this purpose? With a partner, consider the properties of moss, think of a new use for it and make a PowerPoint presentation to share your ideas with the class.

3 Flowering plants

What are the names of the two types of plant stem? How are they different?

Plants that produce seeds are known as flowering plants. There are two groups of flowering plants: **gymnosperms** and **angiosperms**.

- They can live in all types of environment.
- They have vegetative organs that control their vital functions.
- They have reproductive organs that carry out the function of reproduction.
- They do not need a moist environment to reproduce.

3.1 Vegetative organs

The vegetative organs are essential for maintaining life through the function of nutrition. They include the roots, stem, and the leaves.

ROOTS

The roots fix the plant in the ground, as well as absorbing water and minerals from the soil. **Secondary roots** sprout from the **main root**. Secondary roots grow **root hairs** that help to increase the plant's area of absorption.

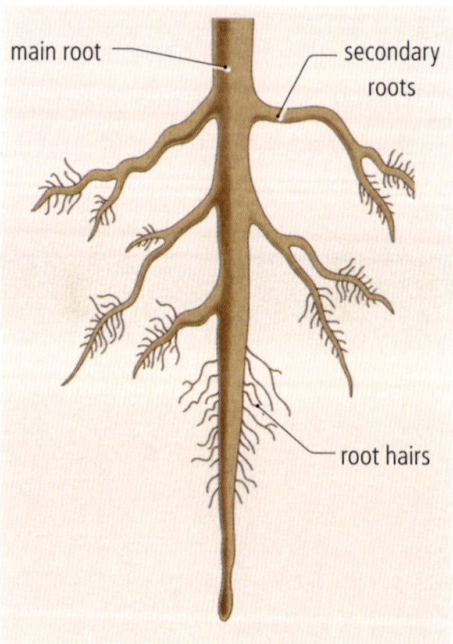

STEM

The stem contains **xylem**, which transports water and nutrients from the roots to all parts of the plant. It also contains **phloem**, which carries nutrients produced in the leaves around the plant. The stem keeps the plant **upright** and can be rigid (**woody**) or flexible (**herbaceous**).

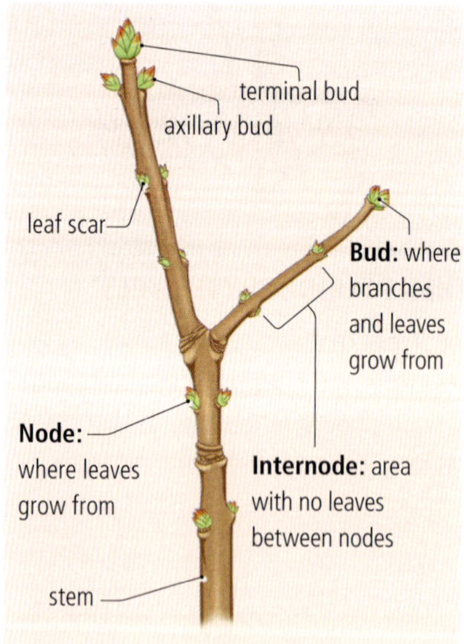

LEAVES

Stomata, the **tiny** green **pores** in green plant leaves, take in carbon dioxide and expel oxygen as part of **photosynthesis** and **gas exchange**. Water travels through the plant and is expelled from the stomata in the process of **transpiration**.

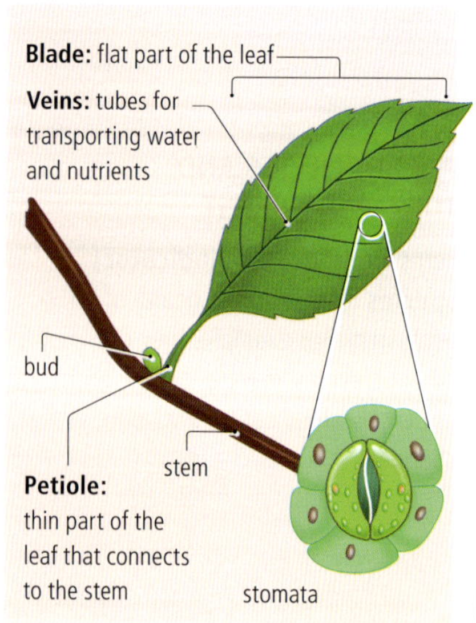

ACTIVITIES

13. Describe the functions of xylem and phloem.

14. Name the three components of roots. Which parts help plants take water from a bigger area?

15. How are woody and herbaceous stems different? Do trees have herbaceous or woody stems? In a local park, classify plant stems as herbaceous or woody. Draw pictures or take photographs of the plants and use the internet to identify the species.

3.2 Gymnosperms

Gymnosperms are a group of flowering trees and bushes that can exist in all types of climate and often form large forests.

Gymnosperm leaves are hard, shaped like **scales** or **needles** and often sharp.

Juniper leaves

Gymnosperm seeds grow in **cones**, not in fruit.

Gymnosperm flowers are small. They don't have petals or sepals. They form **cones**.

A perennial, 'evergreen' forest

Pine flowers

Most gymnosperms are **perennial**: they do not lose their leaves in winter.

GROUP VARIATIONS

Blue spruce leaves have a distinctive blue-grey color.

Ginkos are deciduous and have unique fan-shaped leaves.

Yews have bright red cones that resemble fruit.

Cycads look like palms but are in fact gymnosperms too.

ACTIVITIES

16. Where do gymnosperm seeds grow? What happens when the seeds are mature?

17. Why are ginkos an unusual type of gymnosperm?

18. There are two types of evergreen forest: tropical and temperate. How and why do you think they are different? Choose one of the types and look it up on the Internet. Write one paragraph to explain the most important information you find.

GYMNOSPERM REPRODUCTION

Male gymnosperm flowers form **cones** that produce **pollen**. Female flowers also form cones. The flowers contain **ovules**.

Female larch cone

Reproductive cycle

The wind carries the pollen to the ovules.

The fertilised ovules turn into **pine nuts** (seeds).

Pine nuts

The female cone hardens to protect the seeds. When the seeds are mature the dry cone falls to the ground.

The seeds germinate, new plants grow, and the cycle begins again.

3.3 Angiosperms

Angiosperms are the largest group of flowering plants. The group includes many species of grasses, trees and bushes.

- Angiosperms **reproduce sexually**.
- Flowers are the reproductive organs.
- Flowers can be **hermaphroditic** (containing male and female reproductive organs) or **unisex** (containing only male or female organs).

Hermaphroditic lily plant

Catkins are normally unisex.

The **stamen** is the male reproductive organ. Male sex cells (**pollen**) are produced in the **anthers**.

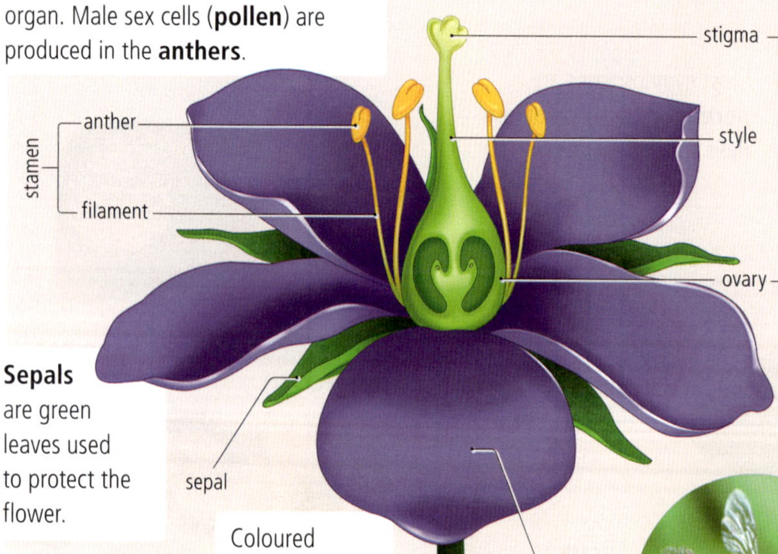

Sepals are green leaves used to protect the flower.

Coloured **petals** attract pollinating insects.

The lower part of the pistil includes the ovary. Female sex cells are produced inside **ovules**.

Pollen is transferred by insects or the wind to the **pistil** – the female reproductive organs.

ANGIOSPERM TYPES

Angiosperms are divided into two groups: monocotyledons and dicotyledons.

Monocotyledon seed embryos have one cotyledon (embryonic leaf). They produce leaves with **parallel veins** and no petiole. They have flowers with three, six or nine parts.

Palm

Wheat

Parallel-veined leaf

Dicotyledons are the bigger group. Seed embryos have two cotyledons. They produce leaves with **branched veins** and flowers of four or five parts.

Holly

Marigold

Branched-veined leaf

ACTIVITIES

19. Describe the differences between hermaphroditic and unisex flowers. Which type do you think is more common?

20. How many parts do monocotyledon flowers have and what is the distinctive characteristic of their leaves?

21. Draw a diagram of the female reproductive organs in angiosperms. In which part is the seed produced?

4 Plant nutrition

> What is phloem sap?

In the process of nutrition, living things obtain the **energy** and **nutrients** they need for maintaining life.

- Human beings and other animals need to take their food from plants and other living things. However, plants are **autotrophs**, meaning they are able to make their own food.
- Plants are not only essential to life on Earth as a form of food: the oxygen (O_2) they expel during the process of photosynthesis makes it possible for living things to breathe. It also consumes the atmosphere's toxic carbon dioxide (CO_2).
- Plant nutrition includes the following steps:

DID YOU KNOW?

Apples, rhubarb and spinach are all healthy foods – but you can have 'too much of a good thing'. Spinach and rhubarb can kill you ... if you eat more than 5kg at once! Apple seeds contain cyanide, a highly toxic substance, but you'd need a whole cup to be in danger – that's probably 200 apples! Can you think of any other poisonous plants?

3 Photosynthesis:

- In the leaves **chlorophyll** absorbs sunlight to collect the necessary solar energy to perform photosynthesis.
- Leaf **stomata** take carbon dioxide from the air and expel oxygen.
- The raw sap is transformed into **phloem sap**.

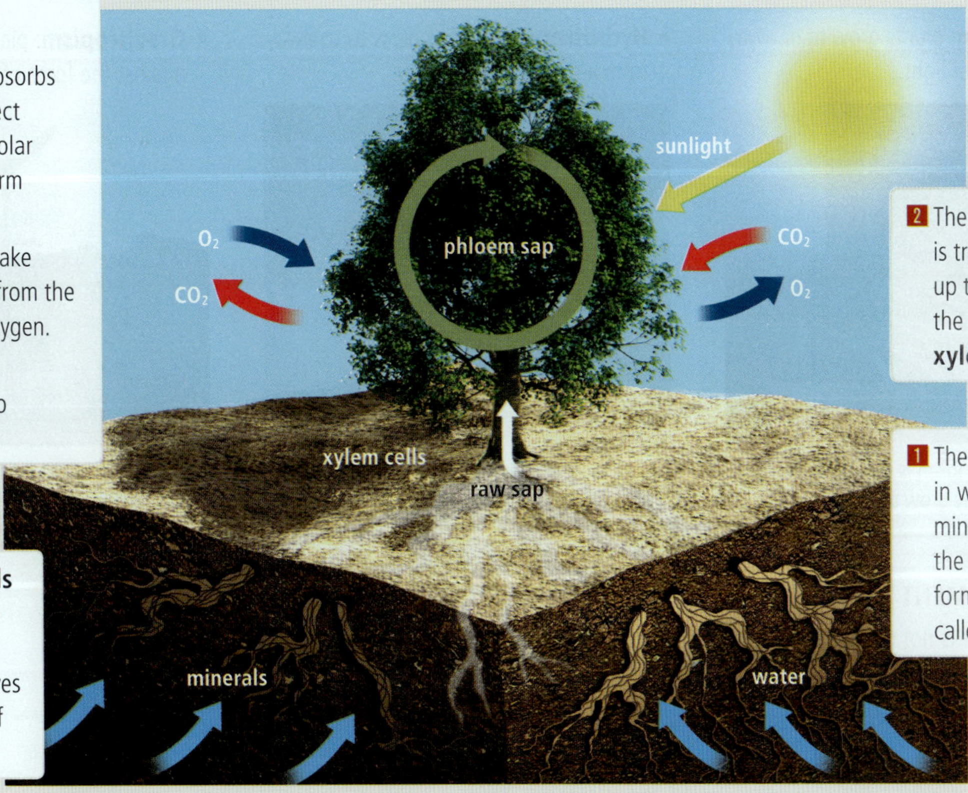

2 The raw sap is transported up the stem to the leaves by **xylem cells**.

1 The roots take in water and minerals from the ground. This forms a mixture called **raw sap**.

4 **Phloem cells** transport the phloem sap from the leaves to all parts of the plant.

ACTIVITIES

22. What is the exchange of gases involved in photosynthesis? Why is this process essential to life on Earth?

23. Describe the steps involved in the transformation of water and minerals into phloem sap.

24. Can plants carry out photosynthesis at night? Explain your answer then research plant respiration. Draw a diagram to illustrate day and night time plant gas exchanges.

5 Interaction and adaptation

➔ How are plants able to move?

5.1 Interaction

Plants are not able to move in the way that other living things can. However, they can respond to **specific external stimuli**. These include: **gravity**, **light** and **water**.

There are two types of interaction: tropism and nastic movement.

TROPISM

This involves movement of the plant's roots, stem or leaves **in relation to the stimulus**. Movement can be:

- **Positive** (towards the stimulus).
- **Negative** (away from the stimulus).

Tropisms have different names depending on the related stimulus:

- **Phototropism**: plants grow to or away from a source of light.

Positive phototropism is present in most plant stems. They grow towards the Sun.

- **Hydrotropism**: plants grow to or away from a source of water.

Roots grow towards water. This is positive hydrotropism.

- **Gravitropism**: plants grow with or against the force of gravity.

In positive gravitropism, plant roots grow towards the centre of the Earth.

NASTIC MOVEMENT

Nastic movement is not dictated by the direction of stimulus. These movements happen more quickly than tropisms. They are not permanent and can also reverse quickly.

Like tropisms, the names of nastic movements also relate to the stimuli involved, for example:

- **Photonasty**: Response to changes in light.

Many plants, including tulips, close their flowers at night.

- **Seismonasty**: Response to touch.

Venus fly traps close their leaves in response to insects landing.

5.2 Adaptation

As well as interacting with their environment, plants also physically adapt to environmental factors, such as **light**, **water** and **minerals**.

- **Climbing plants** climb other plants in search of light.

Liana vines have adapted to the rainforest environment by climbing trees and sending roots down to the ground.

- **Aquatic plants** have adapted to living in water.

Many aquatic plants have little or no strengthening tissue in their stems and leaves. It is not necessary as they are always supported by the water around them.

- **Dry climate plants**, such as **succulents**, can store water inside their stems and leaves. They can also reduce to only their underground parts in very dry weather.

Liquid is stored inside aloe vera leaves.

- **Parasitic and epiphytic** plants live on other plants. Epiphytic plants live on trees only as a way of reaching light, but parasitic plants use their host as a source of necessary water and minerals.

Orchids are epiphytic.

Mistletoe is parasitic.

- **Carnivorous plants** obtain some of their nutrients from eating animals. This is usually because the soil in their environment does not contain enough nitrogen.

The sticky glands of cape sundew trap insects.

ACTIVITIES

25. What are the three stimuli that plants respond to?
26. How do desert plants adapt to their environment?
27. If a house plant grows towards a window, which tropism is the plant exhibiting?
28. Explain the differences between parasitic and epiphytic adaptations. Which adaptation could be harmful to the host plant? Why?
29. Some aquatic plants don't have roots. How are they able to absorb water and minerals? Search the Internet to check your answer.
30. Investigate carnivorous plants: Make a list of different species, then choose one example and write a short report on how they catch and digest animals.

6 Plant reproduction

Why do flowering plants grow fruit?

Because all living things eventually die, it is important for new examples of the same species to grow. Reproduction makes this possible.

There are two types of plant reproduction:

- **Asexual reproduction:** a single plant reproduces itself without the **gametes** (sex cells) of another plant. The new plant is a clone of the original plant.
- **Sexual reproduction:** two gametes are needed (**male** and **female**). The new plant is different from the original plants.

6.1 Asexual plant reproduction

There are many different forms of asexual reproduction in plants, including spore reproduction and vegetative reproduction.

VEGETATIVE REPRODUCTION

Natural vegetative reproduction is common in both herbaceous and woody perennial plants. It allows the plants to survive periods of bad weather and involves different types of stem modification.

Artificial vegetative reproduction carried out by human beings is also common. This allows healthy examples of desirable plants to be reproduced in short periods of time for agricultural purposes.

Types of natural stem modification

Ginger is a **rhizome**: a horizontal stem modification that permits new shoots to grow after a period of bad weather.

Plants, such as strawberries, form **stolons**. These connectors form **adventitious roots** from which new plants grow.

Onions are **bulbs**: shortened stems with leaves. Their purpose is to store food during periods of bad weather.

Plants, such as potatoes, form **tubers** from stolons or rhizomes. They grow near the surface of the Earth.

SPORE REPRODUCTION

Spore cells are present in non-flowering plants like **ferns** and **mosses**. They grow inside **sporangia** that appear during periods of reproduction. When the sporangium opens the spores fall to the ground and new plants can grow if the conditions are favourable.

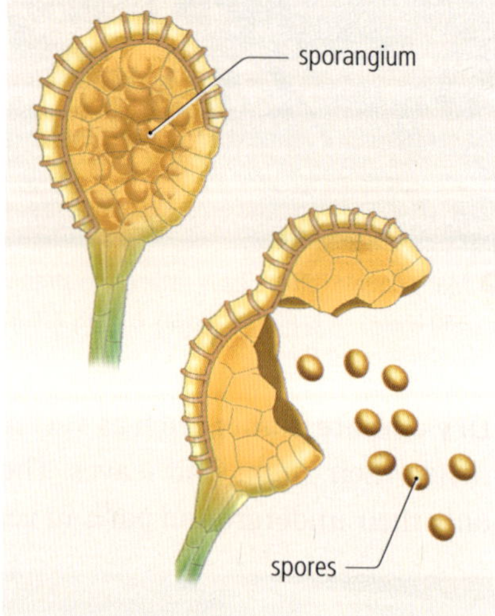

ACTIVITIES

31. Describe the differences between asexual and sexual reproduction in plants. Which type of reproduction is carried out by human beings?
32. Which plant organs have adapted to allow vegetative reproduction? Which modification forms a type of food store?
33. Explain fertilisation in sexual plant reproduction. What does the embryo turn into?
34. How are plant seeds moved from the body of the plant to the ground? Can you think of any other ways that this could happen?

6.2 Sexual plant reproduction

Sexual reproduction in plants requires hermaphrodite or unisex flowers, usually with **brightly-coloured** petals that attract insects. It involves the following processes:

1. Pollination
2. Fertilisation
3. Seed formation
4. Fruit formation
5. Germination

DID YOU KNOW?

Plant reproduction produces one of the fastest growing cells in nature. In some species the pollen tube that grows when the pollen lands on the stigma grows as fast as one centimetre an hour from a single cell. In fact, the pollen tube of a maize plant can grow up to 30 centimetres in one day! Why do you think it has to grow so quickly?

Pollination: pollen is carried from the **male stamen** to the **female pistil**. This can occur between two plants or within one hermaphrodite plant. Pollen is usually transported by insects but can also be blown by the wind.

Fertilisation: the pollen grows a **pollen tube** that allows it to reach the ovule. This results in the male and female gametes mixing, and the formation of an embryo.

Seed formation: the embryo is surrounded and nourished by protective tissue and the seed begins to form.

Fruit formation: in angiosperms the ovary matures and turns into fruit that protects the seeds inside. At this stage the petals and stamen dry and fall from the plant.

Germination: when the fruit is mature it falls from the plant to the ground. With adequate moisture and temperature conditions the seeds can germinate and begin to grow new plants.

ACTIVITIES

35. Think about the fruit you eat. Does it always contain seeds? How can *seedless* fruit be possible? Use the internet to investigate, and then share your discoveries with a partner.

36. Plants that reproduce asexually clone themselves. Why is plant cloning useful to human beings? Can other living things be cloned? What would the advantages and disadvantages of cloning human beings be? Discuss your ideas with a partner.

7 Endangered plants

Why do plants become endangered? Can you think of some endangered species of plant?

Plants can be **endemic** (native) to one place or be distributed across many areas.

If the conditions in an area change, endemic plants are sometimes unable to survive. Human activity causes a number of these changes:

- **Population:** humans take up space once occupied by plant life.
- **Pollution:** air and water supplies are polluted by industry.
- **Introduced species:** ecosystems are changed by the new species.
- **Over consumption:** the increasing world population needs more plants to consume as food.

It is important to protect biodiversity on the Earth so that it can be enjoyed by future generations. Here are some plants that are currently endangered:

This **Monkey-puzzle tree** is native to the Andes. It can live up to 1000 years but is now considered endangered. It has sharp triangular leaves that last for up to 15 years!

Known as the **baseball plant** because of its shape, this South African plant is endangered because of its slow growth and popularity as a garden ornament.

Texas wild rice grows only on the banks of the San Marcos River in Texas. Lowering water levels caused by agriculture mean that there are now only 140 examples of the plant left.

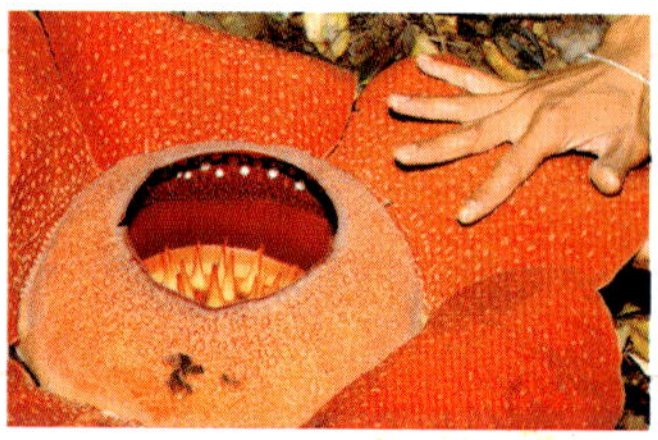

The **Rafflesia flower** is a gigantic parasitic plant, native to Malaysia. It gives off a disgusting smell. The loss of its habitat and pollination problems have made it endangered.

MORE ABOUT ENDEMIC PLANTS

If a species is endemic, it is unique to a particular place, for example a country, region or island. Endemic species are more likely to develop in isolated places, like islands or large bodies of water as there is less possibility for the plant to disperse into other areas.

Agriculture, mining and population growth all destroy endemic plant populations.

Aeonium Urbicum is endemic to the island of Tenerife.

ACTIVITIES

37. Describe the four ways that human beings contribute to endangering plants. Can you see any examples of these activities in your local area?

38. Think about or investigate non-endemic plants. Why are these plants able to survive in different conditions?

39. Investigate endemic plants in your region or country. Are they endangered? Have they adapted to climate conditions? Create a computer database with the information you find.

Discovery techniques

> How can we accurately identify different types of trees?

Identifying trees

AIMS

> Identify tree species from leaf characteristics using a dichotomous key.

PROCEDURE

1. In your notebook, copy the table below:

Sample number	Physical description	Species name	Gymnosperm/ angiosperm

2. Choose a leaf sample and write its number in your table. Study the leaf carefully.
3. Note down the leaf's visible characteristics in your table (consider: shape and form, colour, length, arrangement on the stalk, simple or compound structure).
4. Follow the dichotomous key to identify the tree species. Start with step one of the key and choose the statement that best describes your chosen sample. If the sample is not identified go to the number shown and choose the statement that best describes your sample.
5. Work through the key until your leaf sample is identified.
6. Write down the name of the species in your table. From the characteristics of the leaf, decide if the tree is a gymnosperm or angiosperm. Include this information in your table.
7. Repeat steps 2 to 6 for each leaf sample until you have identified all nine species.
8. Use the internet or a botanical reference book to check your answers.

Dichotomous key

1. Has needles (acicular leaves)........................ go to 2
   Has non-acicular leaves .... go to 5
2. Has bunches of needles joined at the bottom........................ go to 3
   Has simple leaves arranged around a shoot .... **fir tree**
3. Needles are in bunches of 2 to 5........................ go to 4
   Needles are in bunches of 10 to 15. .... **cedar tree**
4. Needles are 2.5 to 5 cm long .... **scots pine tree**
   Needles are 10 to 20 cm long .... **stone pine tree**
5. Has scale-like leaves .... **cypress tree**
   Has broad, flat leaves .... go to 6
6. Has simple leaves (one leaf per vein)........................ go to 7
   Has compound leaves (more than one leaflet per vein)........................ go to 8
7. Has rhomboid (triangular/diamond shaped) leaves........................ **poplar tree**
   Has oval shaped leaves with asymmetrical bases .... **elm tree**
8. Has palmate (hand-shaped) leaves........................ **horse chestnut tree**
   Has pinnate leaves (leaflets grow from several places on the stalk) ..... **ash tree**

MATERIALS

> Numbered leaf samples of fir, cedar, scots pine, stone pine, cypress, poplar, elm, horse chestnut and ash trees.

CONCLUSIONS

1. Did you have any problems using the key? If so, what were they?
2. Choose four different plant samples and make your own dichotomous key to identify them. Try to use different criteria from those used above. Share your key with a partner. Try to identify your partner's plants by using their dichotomous key.

Revision activities

1. Look at the following diagram:

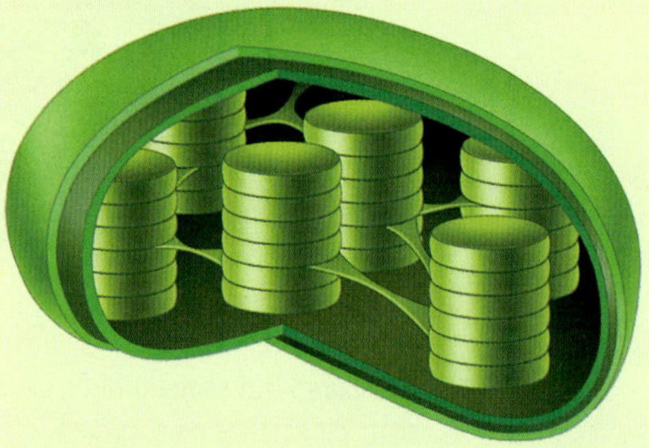

a. Which structure does this diagram represent?
b. What is its function?
c. In which type of cell can this be found?
d. Why are they so important for the environment?

2. Copy the table below. Complete it with the characteristics and types of the main groups of plants.

	non-flowering plants	flowering plants
characteristics		
main groups		

3. Copy and complete the paragraph:

"Angiosperms reproduce sexually through reproductive organs called ..... . These reproductive organs can be ..... , containing male and female reproductive organs, or ..... , containing only male or female organs."

4. Copy and label the following diagram:

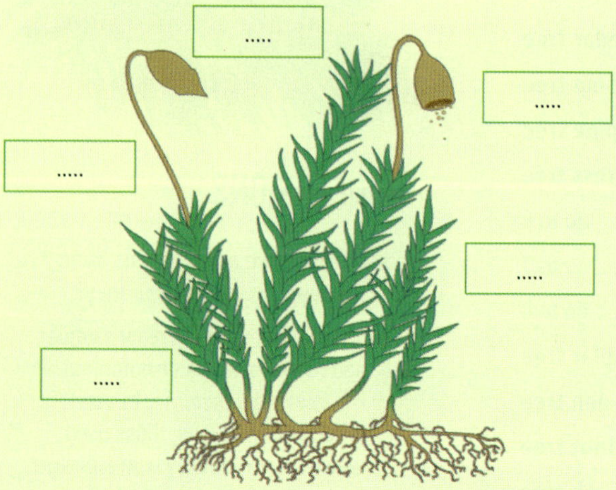

a. What type of plant is shown in the diagram?
b. Why are these plants so important for the environment?

5. Copy the table below. Insert the structures you labelled in Activity 4 and identify their main functions.

structure	function

6. Copy the table and write the following plants in the correct column according to the group they belong to: *pine, orange tree, silver fir, moss, fern, rose, horsehair, daisy, clover, liverworts.*

non-flowering plants	flowering plants

7. Copy and label the following diagram:

a. Which type of plant is shown in the diagram?
b. Why are these plants so important for the environment?
c. Copy the table below, insert the structures from exercise a. and identify their main functions.

structure	function

8. Which type of bryophyte does not have caulidia or phyllidia? How do these plants connect with the ground?

9 Below are some characteristics of different types of plants. Identify the following plant types.

a. The seeds produced by these plants grow inside fruit.
b. These plants have no vascular tissue. They don't have roots, stem or leaves.
c. These plants have vascular tissue. They reproduce using spores.
d. The seeds produced by these plants do not grow inside fruit.

10 Create a mind map describing the reproductive cycle of gymnosperms. You can use different shapes, arrows or colours. The following terms should be included:

male, germinate, female, pollen, flowers, wind, fertilise, cones, new plant, ovules, pine nuts.

11 Angiosperms are the largest group of flowering plants. What are the two groups they are divided into? Write a brief paragraph explaining the main characteristics of each group.

12 Draw a leaf including the main structures that can be identified. Describe their functions and the processes in which they are involved.

13 Copy and label the following diagram and then write a brief explanation of the function of each structure:

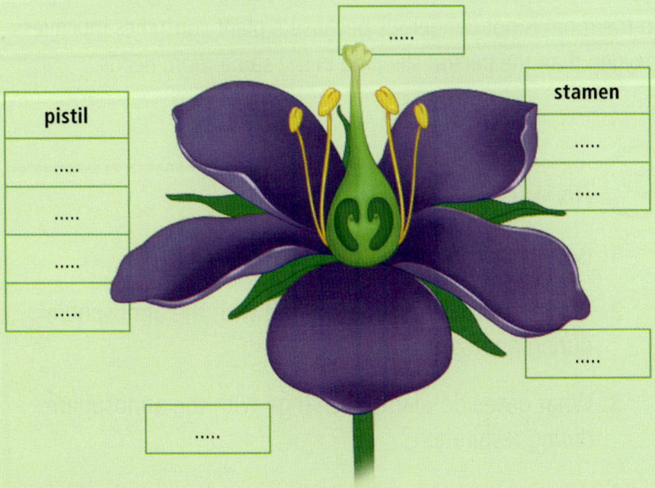

14 In what types of areas are endemic species of plants more likely to develop? Why? What factors put endemic species of plant at risk?

15 Both parasitic and epiphytic plants live on other plants. What is the difference between these two types of adaptation?

16 What is the difference between sexual and asexual reproduction in plants? Draw a diagram explaining all the processes involved in sexual reproduction in plants.

17 The roots, the leaves and the stem are the vegetative organs of flowering plants. They are essential for maintaining life through the function of nutrition. Identify the organ whose function is described in the following sentences:

a. Fix the plant in the ground.
b. Transports water and nutrients from the roots to all parts of the plant.
c. Absorb water and mineral from the soil.
d. Photosynthesis and transpiration take place here.
e. Contain tiny pores where gas exchange takes place.
f. Keeps the plant upright. Can be rigid or flexible.
g. Help to increase the plant's area of absorption.
h. Carries nutrients produced in the leaves around the plant.

18 Answer the following questions about gymnosperms:

a. What types of plant are they?
b. What are gymnosperm leaves like?
c. Where do the seeds grow?
d. What is the meaning of the following sentence? *most gymnosperms are perennial.*
e. What do gymnosperm flowers look like?

19 Plants are able to adapt to the environment. Describe how some plants ...

a. ... adapt to having little water.
b. ... obtain nutrients they can't find in the soil.
c. ... reach light in the rainforests.
d. ... survive when they are surrounded by water.

20 Think about vegetative reproduction:

a. In natural vegetative reproduction, how and why do plants adapt?
b. Which stem modification allows new shoots to grow after periods of bad weather?
c. What type of modification is an onion an example of? What is the purpose of this modification?
d. Which modification grows adventitious roots?
e. From which other two stem modifications are tubers formed?
f. Why is artificial vegetative plant reproduction often carried out by human beings?

Read and think

PLANTS BREATHE TOO

Which gas do plants give off at night?

Plants, like all living things, need to breathe. Respiration is essential for plants to obtain the energy they need to grow, develop and reproduce. It is also necessary for maintaining the overall balance of our planet.

Plant respiration involves an interchange of gases with the atmosphere, in which the plants absorb oxygen and release carbon dioxide.

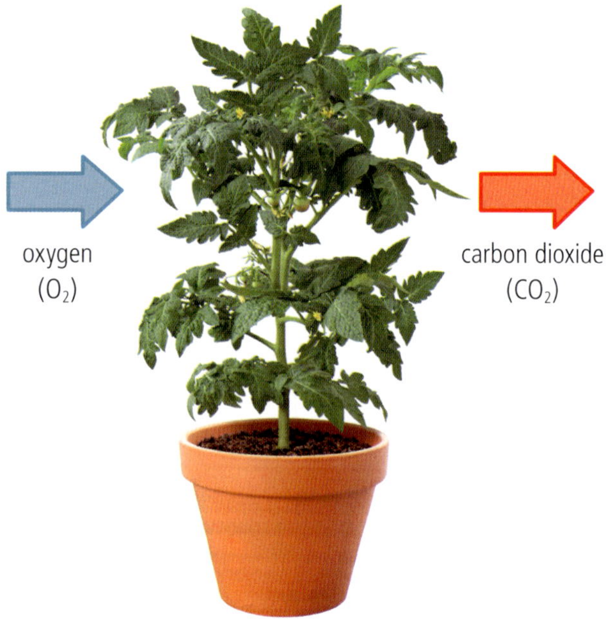

Plants breathe through stomata and lenticels, which are openings on their leaves and stems.

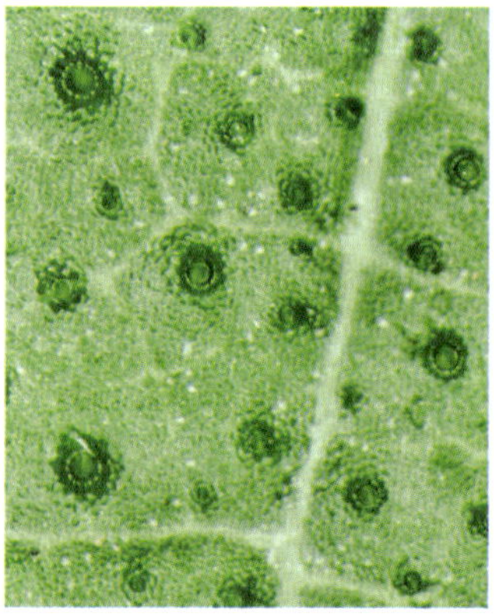

Leaf stomata (magnified) and stem lenticels

Photosynthesis, the process through which plants expel oxygen into the atmosphere, only occurs during the day. On the other hand, plant respiration takes place both during the day and at night. It is a vitally important part of maintaining balance, in terms of both our climate and the gases present in the atmosphere.

During respiration plants absorb oxygen through stomata and lenticels and release the CO_2 they don't need.

You may have heard that it's not a good idea to have a lot of plants in the same room where you sleep. This is because plants take in more oxygen and release more carbon dioxide at night, when they are not performing photosynthesis, although they do breathe throughout the entire day. However, having just one plant in the room is not dangerous because a plant consumes much less oxygen than the person sleeping in the same room needs.

ANSWER THE QUESTIONS

1. Is photosynthesis the same as respiration?
2. What gases do plants exchange with the atmosphere during photosynthesis?
3. What gases do plants exchange with the atmosphere during respiration?
4. When do plants breathe? When do plants perform photosynthesis?
5. What structures do plants use to breathe?
6. Why isn't it advisable to sleep in a closed room with a lot of plants?
7. Why is plant respiration good for the environment?

Work it out

CONCEPT MAP

Use the words in the word cloud to create your own unit map in your notebook. Write any connecting texts you need.

carbon dioxide
needles angiosperms **vegetative organs**
reproduction horsetails nastic movement photosynthesis roots
sexual ferns **Plants** oxygen **plant nutrition**
fruit formation cones leaves seed formation
bryophytes liverworts germination pteridophytes asexual
spore reproduction **flowering**
stem gymnosperms
non-flowering monocotyledons fertilisation **interaction**
mosses tropism vegetative reproduction dicotyledons
pollination

SELF-ASSESSMENT

Carry out a self-assessment of what you learned in this unit. Choose one answer for each question and then check your answers.

1. Which plants do not have vascular tissue?
   a. angiosperms
   b. pteridophytes
   c. bryophytes
2. Which plants produce sori?
   a. Pteridophytes
   b. Bryophytes
   c. Gymnosperms
3. Which plants provide protection from erosion?
   a. Pteridophytes
   b. Angiospermas
   c. Bryophytes
4. Which plants produce cones?
   a. Angiosperms
   b. Bryophytes
   c. Gymnosperms
5. Flowering plants all have ...
   a. roots, a stem and spores.
   b. roots, leaves and tubers.
   c. roots, a stem and leaves.
6. In gymnosperms the female cones harden to protect the ...
   a. pollen.
   b. seeds.
   c. needles.
7. Xylem cells transport ...
   a. phloem sap to all parts of the plant.
   b. raw sap to the leaves of the plant.
   c. raw sap to all parts of the plant.

8. Positive phototropism means that a plant ...
   a. grows away from a source of light.
   b. grows towards a source of light.
   c. grows towards a source of water.
9. Stem modifications allow some plants to reproduce after ...
   a. insect pollination.
   b. the spores fall to the ground.
   c. periods of bad weather.
10. Pollination can occur within one hermaphroditic plant or between two ...
    a. hermaphroditic plants.
    b. unisex plants.
    c. plants (either hermaphrodite or unisex).

04 Invertebrate animals

<< LOOKING BACK

- Which organelles are specific to animal cells?
- What characteristics do all animals share?
- What is the main difference between vertebrates and invertebrates?
- Are all invertebrates able to move from one place to another?
- What groups of invertebrates do the organisms in the images belong to?
- What other groups of invertebrates apart from the ones shown can you name?
- What habitats do the organisms in the images live in? What are the characteristics of those habitats?

A 'Portuguese Man of War'

B Butterfly

C Land snail

Developing and transforming an idea

A great artist has a new idea. She is going to create the most beautiful painting ever – but first the idea needs to grow.

The idea crawls around in the artist's head, feeding off all her experiences. She has been to different places and met interesting people. She has seen other paintings and sculptures, read books, watched films, and listened to music. All that rich material provides fuel for the idea to grow.

The idea gets bigger, stronger and more complicated – but the artist doesn't start painting, not yet. The idea slowly transforms into a plan. What will the shapes be? What colours will it have?

At last, when the plan is finished, the artist explodes into action! The painting emerges, revealing all the beauty contained in the original idea – even though at the beginning, no one could see it.

Ideas are like insects: both develop and transform until they get their final shape ...

?

- What kind of natural process does the text remind you of?
- What vital function is this process related to?
- Can you recognise the stages of this process in the text?
- Could you give an example of an animal, apart from an insect, which goes through this process?
- Do humans undergo this process? Why or why not?

D

Earthworm

LOOKING FORWARD >>

- What different body symmetries do invertebrates have?
- How do sponges obtain their food?
- Are all cnidarians motile?
- Why are annelids also called 'ringed worms'?
- Do all molluscs have an external shell?
- What does the term *arthropod* refer to?
- How do echinoderms breathe?
- What is the largest group of animals on Earth?
- How can we identify and classify arthropods?

1 Invertebrates: general characteristics

➲ What different body symmetries do invertebrates have?

Invertebrates **do not have a backbone**. They are the largest animal group and account for approximately 95% of all animal species on Earth. Jellyfish, sponges, worms, spiders, starfish and butterflies are all invertebrates.

Invertebrates live all over the world in various habitats (marine, freshwater, terrestrial and underground). Some are sessile while others are free-living.

1.1 An invertebrate's body structure

- Many invertebrates have an **external skeleton** or **exoskeleton**. This protects them, gives them shape and keeps them from drying out. Others either have an internal skeleton (starfish) or a soft body with no skeleton (earthworms).
- Invertebrates have three basic types of **body symmetry**.

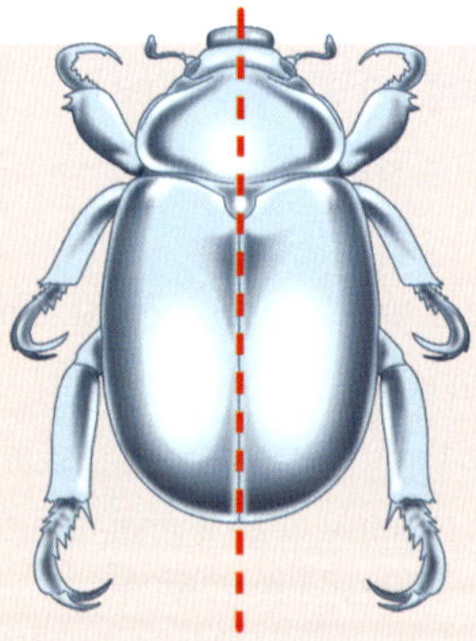

Animals with **bilateral symmetry** can be divided equally along one plane. This plane splits an animal into two mirror-image sides.

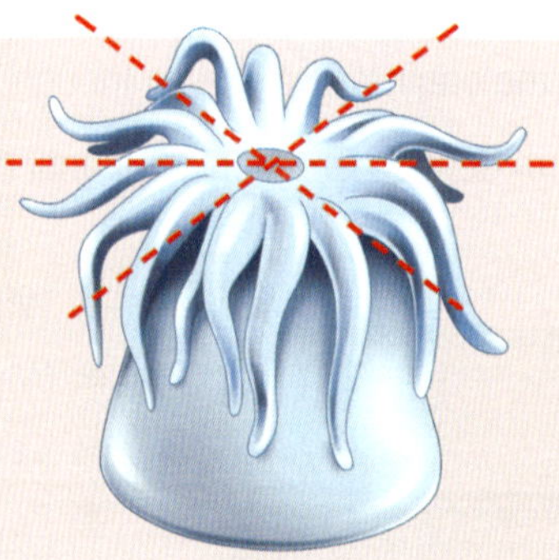

Animals with **radial symmetry** have body parts arranged in a circle around a central axis (usually the mouth). Their bodies can be divided in symmetrical parts along more than one plane.

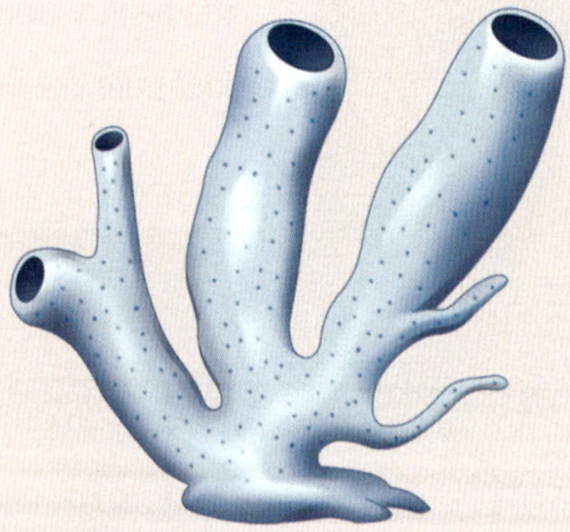

Some invertebrates have an **asymmetrical body**. They are irregular in shape with no symmetry or central axis.

1.2 Vital functions of invertebrates

- Nutrition. Invertebrates can be **carnivorous**, **herbivorous**, **omnivorous**, **filter-feeders**, **parasites**, **active predators**, scavengers or even **saprotrophs**. Their **respiration** can be through the skin (cutaneous), **gills** (branchial), **tracheas** (tracheal) or **lungs**.
- Reproduction. Most invertebrates reproduce **sexually**. They normally have **separate sexes**, but some of them are **hermaphrodites** (they possess both male and female reproductive organs). They are mostly **oviparous**. A few invertebrates reproduce asexually by **fragmentation** or **gemmation**. Some, such as starfish, are also able to regenerate lost body parts. Following reproduction, most invertebrates change shape and appearance by going through a process called **metamorphosis**.
- Interaction. An invertebrate's nervous system and sense organs are usually much simpler than the ones found in vertebrates. Despite this, invertebrates vary greatly in their complexity.

FILTER-FEEDER ORGANISMS

These organisms feed themselves by filtering water through their body and trapping food particles in it. Water also carries the oxygen that these organisms need for respiration, and eliminates their waste products.

CLASSIFYING INVERTEBRATES

PORIFERANS
These are invertebrates with sac-shaped bodies that are full of pores.

CNIDARIANS
These invertebrates have tentacles that are armed with **stinging** cells.

ANNELIDS
These are invertebrates with long cylindrical segmented bodies.

MOLLUSCS
These are invertebrates that have a muscular foot and a shell that is sometimes inside the body.

ARTHROPODS
These are invertebrates that have an external skeleton, a **segmented** body and jointed limbs.

ECHINODERMS
These are invertebrates with an internal skeleton and, in most cases, **spikes**.

DID YOU KNOW?

The largest invertebrate in the world is the **colossal squid** (12–14 m long). It also has the largest eyes in the animal kingdom (27 cm in diameter). These animals can be found in cold waters off the coasts of Antarctica, New Zealand and even some parts of Africa.

Do you know how the colossal squid feeds?

ACTIVITIES

1. Are invertebrates a homogeneous or a heterogeneous group? Justify your answer.
2. Can you recognise the organisms in the photos above? Describe the type of body symmetry each one has. Give one more example of each type of invertebrate.
3. What is the function of a skeleton in invertebrates? Give three examples of an invertebrate with a skeleton and three examples of an invertebrate without one.
4. What groups are invertebrates classified into? Name two invertebrates from each group.
5. Some invertebrates are sessile while others are free-living. Give three examples of sessile invertebrates and three examples of free-living invertebrates.
   a. What environment does each of them live in?
   b. Make a list of advantages and disadvantages of both ways of living.

2 Poriferans

How do sponges obtain their food?

Sponges, also known as **poriferans**, are the most primitive members of the animal kingdom. Their cells are not organised into well-defined tissues and have no organs.

Most sponges are marine animals which may form colonies or live as solitary organisms. Sponges are **sessile**: they attach themselves to the ocean floor and can't move around.

PORIFERAN BODIES

Sponges **lack symmetry** and have an irregular shape.

Their bodies are full of **pores** through which water can circulate. They have a central body cavity (**atrium**) and an upper opening (**osculum**).

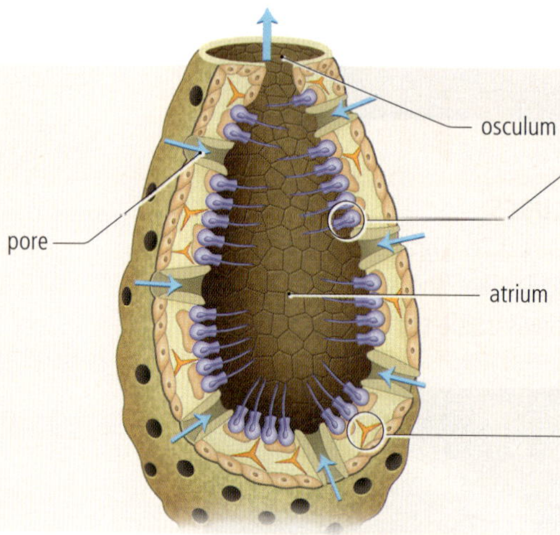

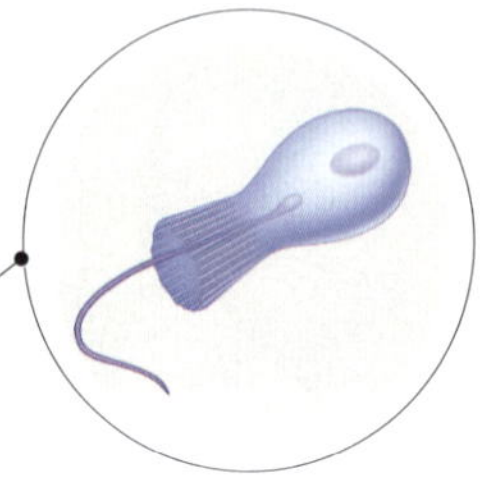

The atrium is lined with flagellated cells called **choanocytes**.

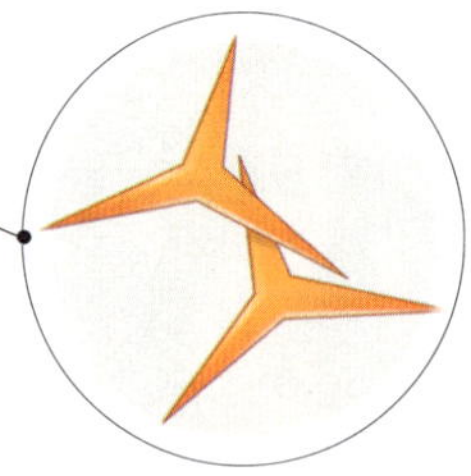

Sponges' skeletons are formed by sharp spikes (**spicules**).

VITAL FUNCTIONS OF PORIFERANS

- **Nutrition**. Sponges are **filter-feeders**. The movement of the flagella on the choanocytes creates a flow of water that circulates through the body. Sponges capture the food particles in the water, and eliminate the waste products through their osculum.
- **Reproduction**. Sponges reproduce both asexually and sexually. Asexual reproduction occurs through **fragmentation** or **gemmation**. In sexual reproduction, sponges release sperm into the water to fertilise the ova, producing **larvae** which have the ability to swim. After some time, they attach themselves to a surface and become individual sessile adults. Most sponges are hermaphrodites.
- **Interaction**. Poriferans have no nervous system or sense organs.

CLASSIFYING PORIFERANS

Sponges are classified into three groups based on the type of spicules they have.

Calcareous sponges have calcium carbonate spicules.

Hexactinellids or 'glass sponges' have silica spicules.

Demosponges have spicules of **spongine** (an elastic protein) and may have silica spicules.

ACTIVITIES

6. What is the function of a sponge's pores? What is the function of its choanocytes?
7. In your own words explain what a filter-feeder is.
8. Look up information about how the natural sea sponges used for bathing are related to poriferans.

3 Cidarians

Are all cnidarians motile?

Cnidarians are a group of aquatic invertebrates which includes jellyfish, sea anemones, hydras and corals. Most cnidarians are marine organisms.

Cnidarians have two basic body forms: **polyp** or **medusa**. Polyps are sessile and may form colonies. Medusae are solitary, motile and float freely.

CNIDARIAN BODIES

A cnidarian's body has a **radial symmetry**. They have a round mouth surrounded by **tentacles** and a digestive cavity (the **gastrovascular cavity**) that acts as a skeleton when it's filled with water. Cnidarians' tentacles have **stinging** cells, called **cnidocytes**. These secrete toxic substances to immobilise prey or for defence.

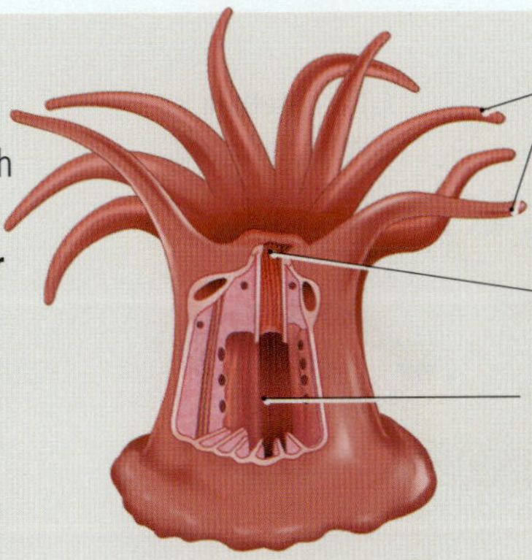

Polyps have sac-like bodies.

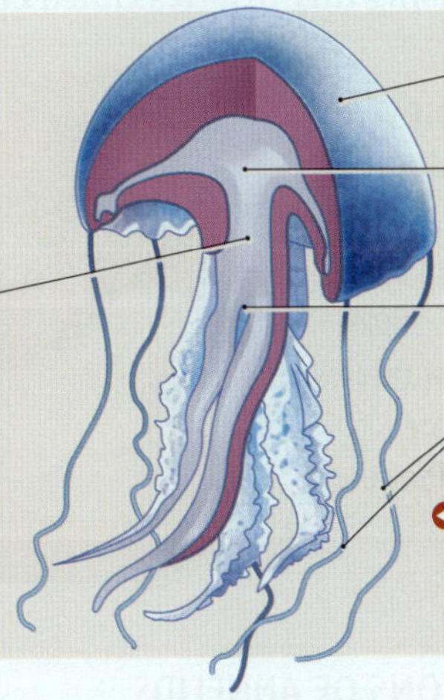

Medusae have umbrella-shaped bodies.

VITAL FUNCTIONS OF CNIDARIANS

- **Nutrition**. Most cnidarians are **carnivores** that capture their prey and digest it in their gastrovascular cavity. Waste is expelled through the mouth. Cnidarians breathe through gas exchange which takes place over their entire body surface.
- **Reproduction**. Polyps reproduce asexually through **gemmation**. Most medusae reproduce sexually.
- **Interaction**. Cnidarians have simple sense organs which allow them to perceive sources of light, detect vibrations and maintain balance.

CLASSIFYING CNIDARIANS

Hydrozoans include marine and freshwater species of cnidarians.

Scyphozoans include most of the common large medusae.

Anthozoans are always polyps. Sea anemones and corals belong to this group.

DID YOU KNOW?

Most people think the Portuguese Man of War is the deadliest jellyfish in the world, but it isn't. In fact, it isn't even a jellyfish. There are two contenders for the prize of 'deadliest jellyfish in the world'. Second place goes to the tiny Irukandji jellyfish, with a poison a hundred times stronger than that of a cobra. But the winner is ... *Chironex fleckeri*, commonly known as 'sea wasp'. Its tentacles contain millions of darts so deadly that, in theory, just one jellyfish (or should it be 'just one dart'?) could kill someone in just 30 seconds ...

Have you ever been stung by a jellyfish?

ACTIVITIES

9. Explain the differences between the body forms of polyps and medusae. In what way are the different body shapes related to the different ways of living?

10. The name *cnidarian* comes from the Greek word *cnidos*, which means 'stinging **nettle**'. What does the name of this group have to do with its characteristics?

4 Annelids

➲ Why are annelids also called 'ringed worms'?

Annelids are worms whose bodies are divided internally into rings or segments called **metameres**. Earthworms and leeches are annelids.

Most annelids are marine organisms, but there are also terrestrial and freshwater species. Some are sessile and live inside underwater tubes, but most move around using tiny **bristles** called **chaetae**.

ANNELID BODIES

Annelids have **bilateral symmetry** and well-developed organs which form specialised organ systems. Some of these organs are repeated in each segment. They don't have a skeleton.

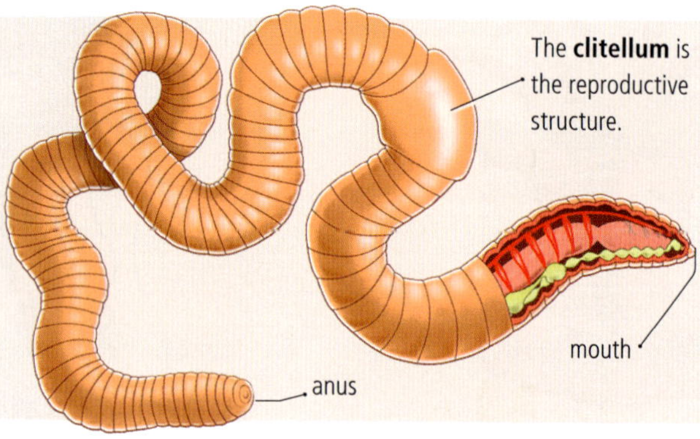

VITAL FUNCTIONS OF ANNELIDS

- **Nutrition**. Annelids can be **predators**, **filter-feeders**, **saprotrophs** (earthworms) or **parasites** (leeches). Aquatic annelids breathe through **gills**, whereas terrestrial annelids breathe through their **skin**.
- **Reproduction**. Annelids reproduce sexually and have **separate sexes**. Some are **hermaphrodites** (earthworms). They are oviparous.
- **Interaction**. Annelids have a specialised nervous system. Their sense organs detect light, vibration and taste.

CLASSIFYING ANNELIDS

Polychaetes, such as Nereis, are marine annelids with many setae.

Oligochaetes have few setae and include all the earthworms.

Hirudineans, such as leeches, have no setae and are parasites.

DID YOU KNOW?

Leeches are blood-sucking parasites, so why would doctors think they might help to cure people? Many centuries ago, people thought that some illnesses were caused by having too much blood. Draining someone's blood could be painful and dangerous, but a leech's saliva contains a natural anaesthetic ... Yuck! In the XIX century leech treatments fell out of popularity, but in the 1970s there was a **revival**. Leech saliva also encourages the flow of blood and stops it from clotting, which can be very useful for delicate microsurgery.

What other things that sound disgusting are actually beneficial to our health?

ACTIVITIES

11. Explain the differences between sponges, cnidarians and annelids in relation to:

a. body symmetry
b. feeding habits
c. reproduction
d. habitat

12. Look for information about the role of an earthworm in the soil ecosystem and write a short report about it.

13. *Annelids have a soft body.* Decide whether this is true or false and explain why.

5 Molluscs

Do all molluscs have an external shell?

Molluscs are a group of animals which includes familiar organisms such as snails, octopuses, squids, clams, slugs, **cuttlefish** and oysters.

Most molluscs are aquatic, generally marine, although there are also freshwater and terrestrial species. Most are **motile**, but some are **sessile** and can stay **latched onto** rocks or other surfaces their whole lives.

MOLLUSC BODIES

Molluscs have **bilateral symmetry** and a soft body which, in general, is divided into a **head**, a **foot** and a **visceral mass**. The **visceral mass** (digestive, respiratory, circulatory and reproductive organs) is surrounded by a membrane called **mantle**. This mantle secretes the shell.

Anatomy of a land snail

VITAL FUNCTIONS OF MOLLUSCS

- **Nutrition**. Molluscs have a complete digestive system. Most molluscs have a rasping tongue with very small teeth called **radula** within their **mouth**. They can be **herbivores** (terrestrial snails), **carnivores** (squid), **filter-feeders** (oysters) and even **parasites** (some sea snails). Aquatic molluscs breathe through **gills** and terrestrial molluscs have **lungs**.
- **Reproduction**. Molluscs perform **sexual** reproduction. Most species have **separate sexes**, but there are also **hermaphrodite** species, such as the land snail. They are **oviparous**.
- **Interaction**. Their sense organs include olfactory, sight, taste and touch organs. Octopuses have highly developed eyes.

ACTIVITIES

14. Explain the characteristics of a mollusc which make it different to other invertebrates.

15. Look up information about the following topics and write a short report.

a. How oysters make pearls.

b. The production of **cultured** pearls on pearl farms.

16. Did you know that some species of land snails are edible?

a. Find information about land snail farms in Spain. Where are they located?

b. What is the technical name for 'snail farming'?

CLASSIFYING MOLLUSCS

GASTROPODS

This group includes slugs, land and sea snails, and limpets. Most are **herbivores**, but some are **carnivores** or parasites.

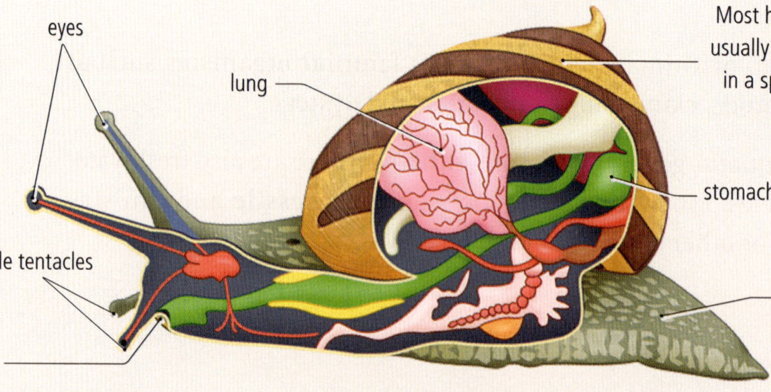

BIVALVES

These include clams, oysters and mussels. They are are **filter-feeders**. Bivalves have no head and their sense organs are located on the mantle margin. They also lack a radula.

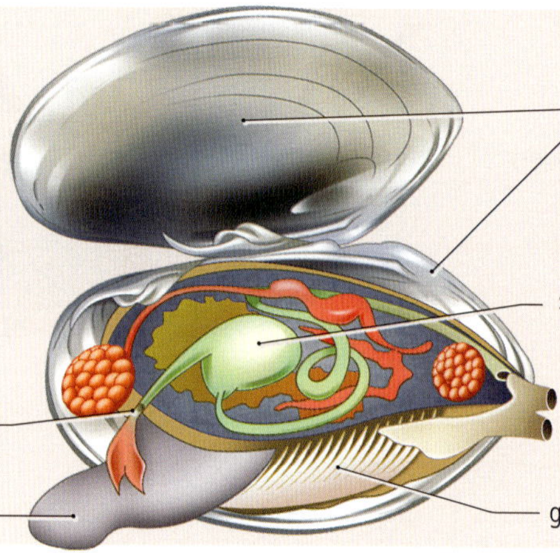

CEPHALOPODS

These include squids, octopuses and cuttlefish. They are **carnivorous predators** which trap their prey using their tentacles.

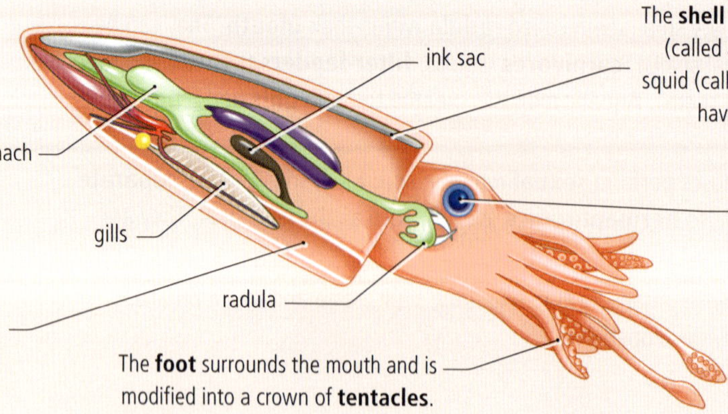

ACTIVITIES

17. What different groups are molluscs classified into? Make a table showing the similarities and differences between the groups of molluscs.

18. What is the function of a cuttlebone in cuttlefish? Explain what other types of molluscs have instead of it. Find out why the cuttlebone is often given to birds such as parrots and cockatoos.

19. Make a list of the different types of molluscs you can find at a fish market. What groups do they belong to?

6 Arthropods

What does the term *arthropod* refer to?

Arthropoda is the largest and most diverse group of animals on Earth. It includes both aquatic and terrestrial organisms. Prawns, spiders, millipedes, butterflies, grasshoppers, ants and flies belong to this group. The word *arthropod* literally means 'jointed limbs'.

ARTHROPOD BODIES

Arthropods have **bilateral symmetry**. Their body is divided into segments that group in most cases to form three parts: the **head**, the **thorax** and the **abdomen**. In some cases the head and the thorax are fused together to form a **cephalothorax**. The body is covered by a **hard articulated exoskeleton** composed of different pieces that fit together.

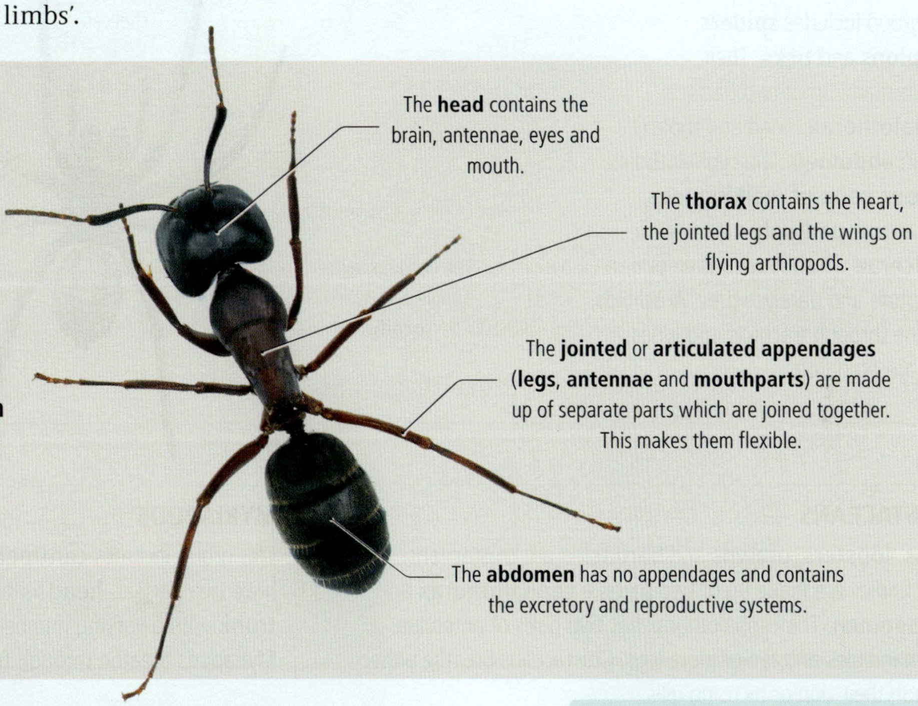

VITAL FUNCTIONS OF ARTHROPODS

- **Nutrition**. Most arthropods are **herbivores**, but there are also **carnivores** and **omnivores**. Some, such as fleas, **ticks** and **lice**, are **parasites**, while others, such as houseflies are **scavengers** (they feed on dead or decaying matter). Aquatic arthropods breathe through **gills**, whereas terrestrial arthropods breathe using **tracheae**. Tracheae are a system of branching tubes that carry oxygen to the entire body.
- **Reproduction**. Arthropods reproduce **sexually**. They have separate sexes and fertilisation takes place internally, inside the female's body. They are **oviparous**. Arthropods **moult** when their bodies become too large for their exoskeletons. That means they shed their exoskeleton and create a larger one to take its place. Some species of arthropods develop through a process called **metamorphosis**, which means 'transformation' or 'change of shape'.
- **Interaction**. Arthropods have a highly developed nervous system. They also have well-developed sense organs including simple eyes (**ocelli**), **compound eyes** and antennae. **Sensitive hairs** detect vibration, taste and touch.

Compound eyes of insects are made up of multiple units (**ommatidia**) each of which functions as a separate visual receptor.

ACTIVITIES

20. How can arthropods grow if they are enclosed in a rigid exoskeleton? Look for information about this, and briefly explain the process.

21. Both arthropods and vertebrates have articulated skeletons which allow one part of the body to move in relation to another. Make a list of the characteristics that make them different.

6.1 Classifying arthropods

Arthropods are classified into four main groups depending on the type and number of their appendages: **arachnids**, **crustaceans**, **myriapods** and **insects**.

ARACHNIDS

This group includes **spiders**, **scorpions** and **ticks**. Their body is made up of two parts: a **cephalothorax** (head and thorax) and an **abdomen**. The cephalothorax has **four pairs of walking legs**, two sensory **pedipalps**, and two **chelicerae** which may contain poison to capture and paralyse prey. Arachnids breathe through tracheas and lungs. They are predators.

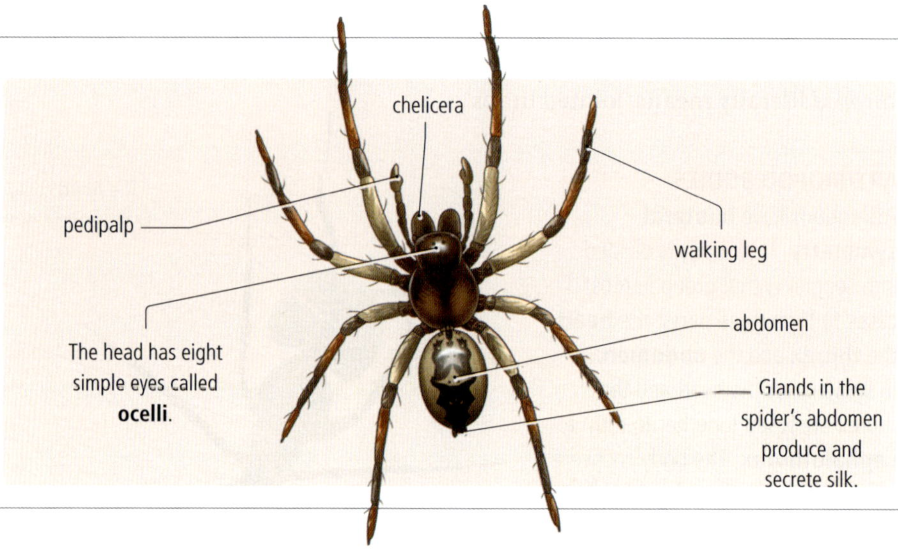

CRUSTACEANS

Crabs, **lobsters**, **prawns** and **barnacles** are crustaceans. Their bodies are made up of two parts: a **cephalothorax** and an **abdomen**. The cephalothorax has two pairs of antennae, two mandibles and ten or more legs. Crustaceans breathe either through their skin or by using gills.

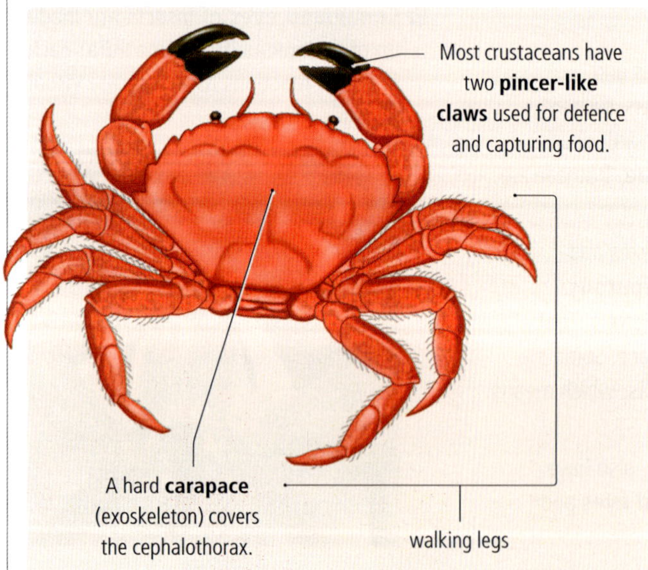

MYRIAPODS

This group includes **centipedes** and **millipedes**. Their bodies have two parts: a **head** with a pair of antennae and an elongated **trunk** with a varying number of segments (from 15 to 200). Myriapods breathe through tracheas.

Centipedes have one pair of legs per segment and a pair of venom claws.

Millipedes have two pairs of legs per segment.

ACTIVITIES

22. What are the main differences between a spider and a crab? What are the similarities between them?

23. Make a list of the different types of crustaceans you can find at a fish market.

24. Spiders produce different types of silk in different glands. Look up information about what spiders use silk for.

25. Make a list of the characteristics that make an arthropod different from other invertebrates.

INSECTS

These are the largest group of invertebrates and the only ones that can fly. Most of them are terrestrial. Their bodies are divided into three parts: the **head**, the **thorax** and the **abdomen**. Insects breathe through a network of tiny tubes called tracheae. In aquatic insects, however, the larvae breathe through gills. Insects grow and develop throughout a process called **metamorphosis**, which can be **complete** or **incomplete**.

GROUPS OF INSECTS

Coleopterans (beetles and ladybirds)

Dyctiopterans (mantis and cockroaches)

Dipterans (flies and mosquitoes)

Lepidopterans (butterflies and moths)

Hymenopterans (wasps, bees and ants)

Odonates (dragonflies and damselflies)

Orthopterans (crickets and grasshoppers)

Hemipterans (cicadas and aphids)

Dermapterans (earwigs)

BIG THINKER

Even when he was a child, **Charles Darwin** was a collector. He loved to collect different minerals, insects, coins, animal shells, stamps, and other bits and pieces. However, he didn't study the things he found ... at least not then. At Cambridge University, Darwin's childhood passion fuelled a new hobby: collecting beetles. Instead of visiting his girlfriend during the winter break, he would stay in order to hunt for more **specimens**! Later in life, Darwin's obsession continued with his study of earthworms, and how orchids manipulate insects into pollinating them.

What do you collect and why?

ACTIVITIES

26. Explain the main differences between arachnids and insects.

27. Insects are also called *hexapods* which means 'six legs'. On this basis, explain why the following organisms can or cannot be considered insects: *spider, crab, grasshopper, centipede* and *scorpion*.

28. What are infestations? Look up information about them and find out what type of invertebrates cause the most common infestations.

7 Echinoderms

How do echinoderms breathe?

Echinoderms are marine animals whose name means 'spiny skin'. Common examples of echinoderms are **starfish** and **sea urchins**.

ECHINODERM BODIES

Adult echinoderms have **radial symmetry**. They do not have a head and their body can usually be divided into **five parts**. Their skeleton is internal (**endoskeleton**). It is made up of **limestone plates** and, in most cases, **spikes**.

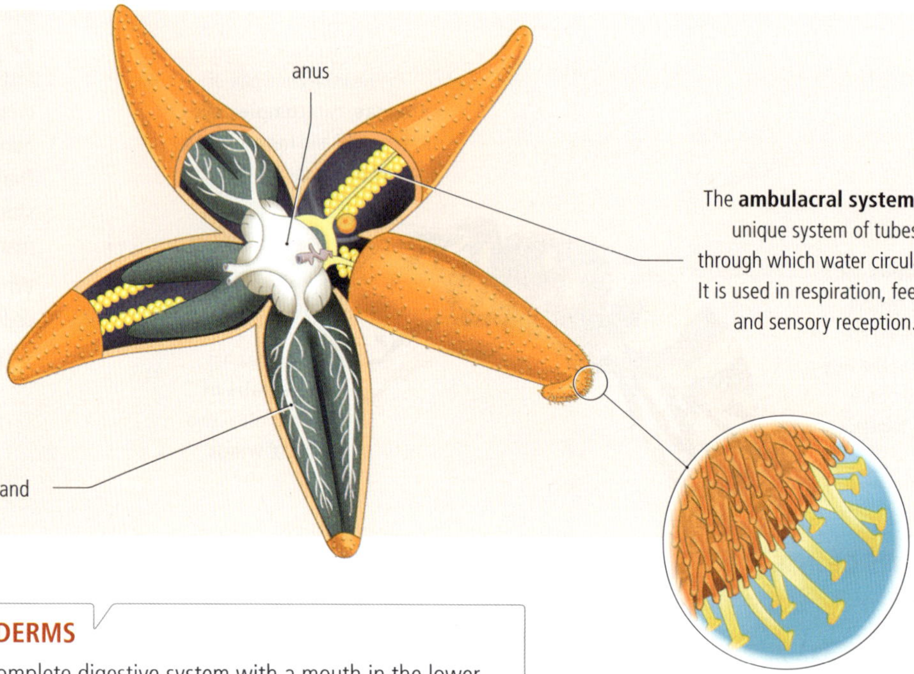

The ambulacral system has external extensions (**tube feet**) with suckers for locomotion.

VITAL FUNCTIONS OF ECHINODERMS

- **Nutrition**. Echinoderms have a complete digestive system with a mouth in the lower part of the animal. They can be carnivores (starfish), herbivores (sea urchins), filter-feeders (feather stars) or scavengers (sea cucumbers). Respiration takes place through small gills and the ambulacral system.
- **Reproduction**. They reproduce **sexually** and **have separate sexes**. Some, like starfish, can reproduce **asexually** by **regenerating** body parts that have been lost.
- **Interaction**. Most echinoderms are sessile or slow moving. They use their tube feet to stick to the ground or for movement.

CLASSIFYING ECHINODERMS

Asteroids (starfish) have five arms.

Echinoids (sea urchins) have globe-shaped bodies covered with spikes.

Holothurians (sea cucumbers) have a cylindrical body.

Crinoids (sea lilies) spend their lives attached to the bottom of the sea.

ACTIVITIES

29. Describe the body structure of an echinoderm. Do a drawing indicating the different body structures.

30. Look for more information about how a starfish regenerates and write a short report about it.

8 Diversity of invertebrate animals

What is the largest group of animals on Earth?

Invertebrates are the most successful and **prolific** animals on the planet. They have adapted to occupy practically every habitat. That's why when we talk about 'biodiversity' we are inevitably also talking about invertebrates.

8.1 How do invertebrates adapt to their environment?

Invertebrate animals adapt to the conditions of the habitats in which they live. There are two major types of habitat: **terrestrial** (land) and **aquatic** (fresh water and marine). Living conditions are different in each environment, and therefore, so is the way these animals adapt.

Invertebrates adapt in a wide range of ways to survive. There are **breathing** and **feeding adaptations**; adaptations for protecting against predators or catching prey, such as **camouflage** and **mimicry**; adaptations for moving or attaching themselves to the substrate; etc.

An arthropod's exoskeleton provides a waterproof layer to prevent water loss in terrestrial environments.

A sponge's body has adapted to achieve maximal efficiency of water flow in order to allow for gas exchange.

Earthworms have strong muscles for crawling and burrowing.

A convolvulus hawk-moth blends into the tree trunk (camouflage) to avoid its predators.

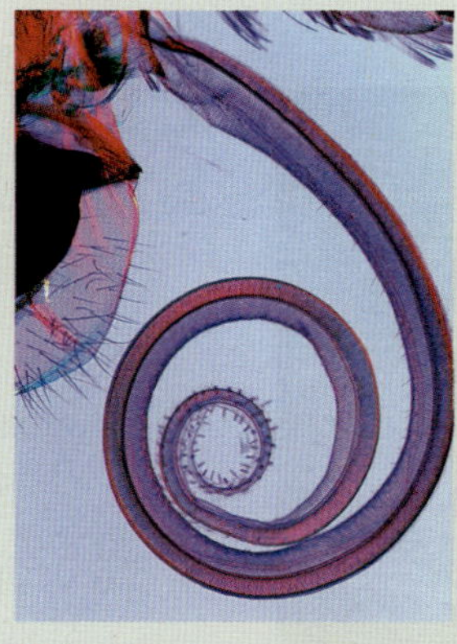

The mouth parts of butterflies consist of a spiral-shaped sucking proboscis. This is used to suck the nectar from flowers.

Mussels attach themselves to stones or shells with the help of strong threads. These are known as the mussel's 'beard'.

ACTIVITIES

31. Explain what the following adaptations are for:
    - a. a bubble of air in aquatic insects such as diving beetles
    - b. stinging cells in medusae
    - c. insects that look like a leaf in shape and colour
    - d. mouth parts adapted to form a biting apparatus in mosquitoes
    - e. chaetae in annelids
    - f. insects that adapt to the colours of their surroundings
    - g. ink in cephalopods

8.2 Beneficial and harmful invertebrates

Some invertebrate species can be **harmful** to humans. Many of the world's most dangerous parasites are invertebrates (ticks, fleas, bed bugs, leeches). Others, such as mosquitoes and flies, transmit a number of diseases caused by infectious agents or cause **plagues** and **pests** (**locusts**, cockroaches).

However, invertebrates are **beneficial** too. Dragonflies, ladybirds and spiders feed on insects and help keep their populations under control. Leeches are useful in medicine. Worms recycle waste and help fertilise soil. Some molluscs are detritus feeders, and therefore clean up their surroundings.

By feeding on flowers' nectar bees help in the process of plant pollination.

Coral reefs support a myriad of life forms aside from being living organisms themselves.

Plagues of locusts are **devastating** natural disasters that have been feared throughout history.

8.3 Are invertebrates in danger of extinction?

The actual number of invertebrate species is unknown, but it is thought that there may be tens of millions of invertebrates, the vast majority of them being insects.

Despite the fact that new species of invertebrates are being discovered regularly each year, invertebrates are at risk from a variety of threats. According to the Red List of Threatened Species, one fifth of the world's invertebrates may be heading for extinction.

Rosalia longicorn or *Rosalia alpina* is an endangered beetle that feeds on dead wood. They live in beech woodlands in northern Spain.

The endangered lepidopteran Spanish moon moth (*Graellsia isabellae*) eats pine tree needles.

ACTIVITIES

32. Make a list of invertebrates that are beneficial to humans and another list of harmful invertebrates. In each case, explain the reason for your choice.

33. Decide whether the following statement is true or false and explain why.

Some species of invertebrates might become extinct before scientists know that they have even existed.

Discovery techniques

IDENTIFYING INVERTEBRATES

How can we identify and classify arthropods?

Dichotomous key for classifying invertebrates

1. Asymmetrical body .... **sponges**
   Symmetrical body .... go to 2
2. Radial symmetry .... go to 3
   Bilateral symmetry .... go to 4
3. Has an internal skeleton .... **echinoderms**
   Hasn't got an internal skeleton .... **cnidarians**
4. Segmented body .... go to 5
   Non-segmented body .... **molluscs**
5. Has an exoskeleton .... **arthropods**
   Hasn't got an exoskeleton .... **annelids**

Dichotomous key for classifying arthropods

1. Body made up of two or three parts .... go to 2
   Body made up of many body segments .... go to 3
2. Body made up of two parts .... go to 4
   Body made up of three parts; three pairs of legs .... **insects**
3. Cylindrical body; two pairs of legs on each body segment .... **millipedes**
   Flat body; one pair of legs on each body segment .... **centipedes**
4. Eight legs .... **arachnids**
   Ten or more legs .... **crustaceans**

ACTIVITIES

1. Make a list of the criteria used to classify invertebrates in the dichotomous key above. Explain each of them.
2. Identify the criteria used to classify arthropods in the dichotomous key above. Explain each of them.
3. Make your own dichotomous key to classify the following organisms using the suggested criteria in each case:
   a. molluscs (type of shell)
   b. arthropods (number of legs)
4. Decide whether the following criteria are or are not suitable for classifying the mentioned organisms. Give reasons for your answer in each case.
   a. echinoderms (symmetry)   b. molluscs (presence of a radula)
5. Read the following description. What type of invertebrate is being referred to?
   Radial symmetry; internal skeleton; five or more arms

Revision activities

1. Explain how invertebrates can survive without bones. Give two different examples of invertebrates to support your argument.

2. Say if the following sentence is true or false. If it is false, explain why:

   All invertebrates are parasites and are able to regenerate lost body parts.

3. Some scientists believe that bilateral symmetry is better adapted for movement, whereas radial symmetry is better for sessile organisms. With a partner, discuss why this may be correct. Then, discuss whether asymmetrical, radial, or bilateral symmetry is better for sessile organisms. Give a reason for your choice.

4. As you know, sponges are filter-feeders. With the help of flagella, food and oxygen are filtered out of the water and digested. But what happens if the water they are filtering is dirty or sandy? Search for information on the Internet to find out how a sponge protects itself in polluted water.

5. Sponges and corals can look superficially similar. At times scuba divers have trouble telling them apart! First, label each picture as a sponge or a coral. Then, fill in the following chart to explain the similarities and differences between them. Add your own category at the end to compare or contrast the two organisms.

A

B

	sponges	corals
group of invertebrates		
presence/absence of sense organs		
body symmetry		
type of reproduction		
feeding habits		
.....	.....	.....

6. Decide whether the following sentence is true or false, and explain why.

   All annelids are mobile organisms that live underwater.

7. Some scientists are now studying sea sponges to predict global warming and other changes in the marine environment. Look for information on why researchers are using poriferans in this way.

8. Identify what group of molluscs (*gastropods, bivalves, cephalopods, or a combination of the three*) the following sentences refer to. Justify your answer.
   a. This group is most likely to be found in the woods.
   b. This group has tentacles.
   c. Members of this group lack a head.
   d. These groups are most likely to be found on a dinner plate.
   e. This group produces pearls.

9. Explain the main differences between gastropods, bivalves, and cephalopods based on their shells.

10. Some molluscs, such as land snails, secrete mucus from their strong muscular foot in order to provide suction and move around. Search for additional information about how mucus helps molluscs.

11. Briefly explain the ecological and economic importance of molluscs.

12. How many parts is an arthropod's body divided into? Describe the general morphology of each of them. Can arthropods be considered *segmented* animals? Justify your answer.

13. Explain how aquatic arthropods breathe. Then, explain how this differs from the way terrestrial arthropods perform respiration.

14. Give examples of invertebrates that live in deserts. What adaptations do they have to survive in this harsh environment? Find out information and write a short report about this topic.

15. Describe what happens to arthropods during moulting. Give examples of invertebrates that undergo this change.

16. One of the ways arthropods have evolved since they first appeared is that they have jointed appendages. With a partner, discuss what the advantages of jointed appendages are.

17 Based on what you know, classify the organisms below. Explain the characteristics you used to classify them.

A 

B 

18 As the human population continues to grow, actions such as deforestation, conventional farming, and widespread pesticide use has led to a decrease in the number of arthropods. Search on the Internet for information about one endangered arthropod and write a short report about it. Make sure to include where it lives and why it is endangered.

19 At first glance, a millipede and an earthworm seem to share many features. Complete the table to compare the two animals. Do you think they are related?

	millipedes	earthworms
kingdom		
group of invertebrates		
symmetry		
reproduction		
habitat		
number of legs		
presence of a skeleton		

20 Say if the following sentences apply to *crustaceans*, *arachnids*, *myriapods*, or *insects*:

a. They often live in a society.
b. Despite being usually found in marine habitats, some species are terrestrial.
c. They are predators.
d. Some members of this group have silk glands.
e. These arthropods can have up to 200 segments.
f. Members of this family include scorpions, mites, and ticks.
g. This group has a three-parts body.
h. They are the only arthropods that may have two pairs of wings.
i. They don't have any antennae.

21 What is the main difference between complete metamorphosis and incomplete metamorphosis?

22 Explain how echinoderms move. How does this differ from sponges?

23 An echinoderm called a 'brittle star' has a unique way of protecting itself from predators. Search for more information on the 'brittle star' and explain what it does when attacked.

24 What do oysters, earthworms, sponges, and feather stars all have in common?

25 The northern walking stick (*Diapheromera femorata*) is an insect that resembles a stick or tree branch. It has camouflage which allows it to remain hidden from a predator's watchful eye. Look for information on the northern walking stick.

a. What physical adaptations help them survive?
b. Name two other invertebrates that use adaptations to hide from predators.

26 Give three examples of how invertebrates help ecosystems. Then, say which of these actions you benefit from in your everyday life.

27 Numerous invertebrates, including sponges, corals, sea urchins, and many molluscs, live in aquatic habitats. With a partner, discuss why it is important to provide safe and healthy conditions for these organisms. Then, make a list of various ways to keep our oceans clean.

28 Match the following terms to their etymological origin:

Molluscs, Annelids, Arthropods, Insects, Echinoderms, Poriferans, Cnidarians

a. Latin for 'six legs'
b. Latin for 'stinging nettle'
c. Latin for 'soft body'
d. Latin for 'joint' and 'foot'
e. Latin for 'little rings'
f. Latin for 'bearing pores'
g. Latin for 'spiky skin"

Read and think

METAMORPHOSIS IN INSECTS

Metamorphosis is the process by which insects and other animals develop and grow. Metamorphosis literally means 'transformation' or 'change of shape'. Metamorphosis in insects can be complete or incomplete. The two types differ in the number of life cycle stages.

INCOMPLETE METAMORPHOSIS

This has three stages. A young insect, called a **nymph**, hatches from an **egg**. The nymph is the eating and growing stage. It moults in order to grow. After several moults, it eventually becomes an **adult**. Adults are the reproductive stage. The females lay eggs and the cycle begins again. Grasshoppers, dragonflies, mantises and cockroaches develop this way.

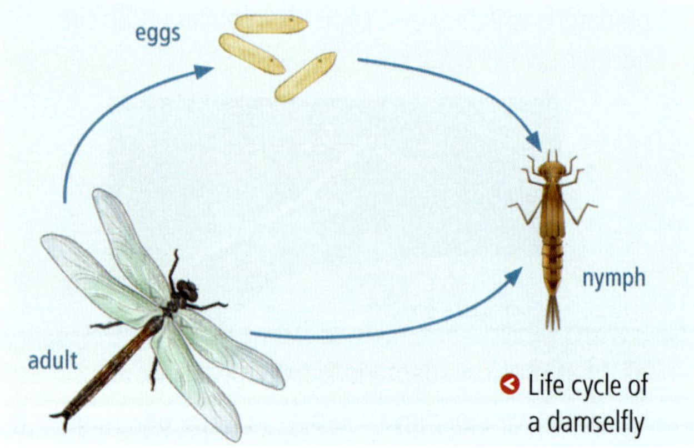

Life cycle of a damselfly

COMPLETE METAMORPHOSIS

This has four stages. The **larva** (caterpillar) hatches from the **egg**. It is the eating and growing stage, and forms a **pupa** or **chrysalis** when it has finished growing. The pupa is, apparently, a passive stage. However, inside the pupa the body re-arranges and eventually it emerges as an **adult**. Adults are the reproductive stage. The females lay eggs and the cycle begins again. This is the way butterflies, moths, bees, flies, beetles and ants develop.

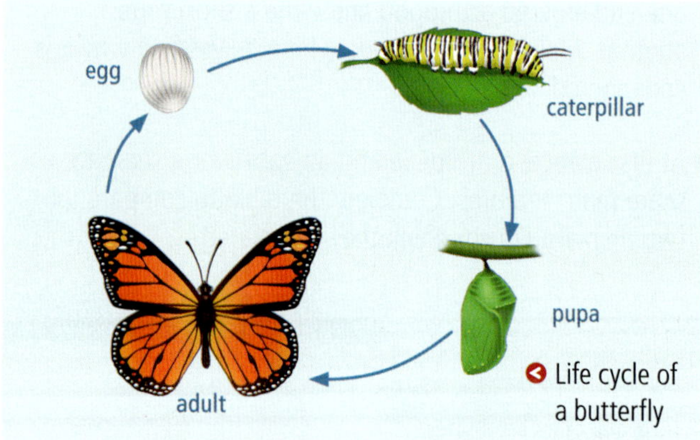

Life cycle of a butterfly

Insect species have adapted to carry out their life cycle in a wide variety of environments. Mosquitoes carry out their larval and pupal stages in water, while crickets undergo their transformation underground. Some larvae are herbivorous, whereas others are carnivorous, or even parasitic. The larva of the common housefly (*Musca domestica*) feeds on any decaying matter, especially dead flesh, whereas bee larvae eat bee milk and beebread, which are made by worker bees. In incomplete metamorphosis, usually nymphal and adult stages have similar feeding habits.

ANSWER THE QUESTIONS

1. Look at the two types of metamorphosis and, in each case, identify: the eating and growing stage, the reproductive stage, and the changing stage.
2. What other groups of animals develop through metamorphosis? Choose one of them and describe its life cycle.
3. Look for information about the social structure in a beehive. What are the functions of the different members in a community of bees?
4. Make a list of the differences in development and growth between humans and insects.

Work it out

Use the words in the word cloud to create your own unit map in your notebook. Write any connecting texts you need.

cnidarians gastropods arthropods snails polychaetes clams hexactinellids anthozoans leeches demosponges cephalopods scorpions myriapods **invertebrates** molluscs hydrozoans sea anemones centipedes wasps bivalves earthworms crustaceans hirudineans poriferans arachnids corals calcarean sponges octopuses lobsters scyphozoans oligochaetes annelids insects

Carry out a self-assessment of what you learned in this unit. Choose one answer for each question and then check your answers.

1. Invertebrates ...
   a. have no backbone or limbs.
   b. don't have sense organs.
   c. have diverse feeding habits.
2. The large central cavity in sponges is called a/an ...
   a. osculum.
   b. gastrovascular cavity.
   c. atrium.
3. Aquatic invertebrates with a mouth surrounded by tentacles and stinging cells are called ...
   a. cephalopods.
   b. cnidarians.
   c. coleopterans.
4. Earthworms and leeches are ...
   a. polychaetes.
   b. annelids.
   c. parasitic worms.
5. Most molluscs have ...
   a. an external shell.
   b. an internal shell divided in two valves.
   c. a shell secreted by their mantle.
6. Crustaceans ...
   a. are terrestrial arthropods.
   b. breathe through gills or their skin.
   c. both a and b
7. A spider's body ...
   a. is divided into a cephalothorax and an abdomen.
   b. has radial symmetry.
   c. has an internal skeleton.
8. Most echinoderms move around using ...
   a. tube feet.
   b. a muscular foot.
   c. jointed legs.
9. Some insects develop complete metamorphosis to ...
   a. grow and eat.
   b. lay eggs and change shape.
   c. grow and develop.
10. Some invertebrates ...
    a. are in danger of extinction.
    b. are beneficial to humans.
    c. both a and b

05 Vertebrate animals

<< LOOKING BACK

- What makes vertebrates different from invertebrates?
- What groups are vertebrates classified into?
- Can you recognise the animals in the images? What group of vertebrates do each of them belong to?
- What environment do most of the vertebrates in each group live in?
- How do vertebrates move?

A B C

Nessie: a living fossil or a hoax?

The real world is an interesting place, but wouldn't it be even more fun if there were ghosts, or aliens, or ... monsters?

In 1933, a legend was born with claims that a gigantic prehistoric animal was living in Loch Ness, a lake in northern Scotland. The same year, a motorcyclist described seeing something like a plesiosaur on a moonlit night – but these aquatic reptiles first appeared about 200 million years ago, and became extinct 66 million years ago. How could one of them still be alive?

Soon, two blurry photographs were taken of Nessie swimming: one seemed to be of a four-legged animal, the other – the most famous of all – showed a small head on a long thin neck, emerging from the water. More 'evidence' was collected over the years but Nessie is now considered by scientists to be a hoax. Yet people still visit the loch, hoping to discover an impossible truth waiting in the cold, calm water ...

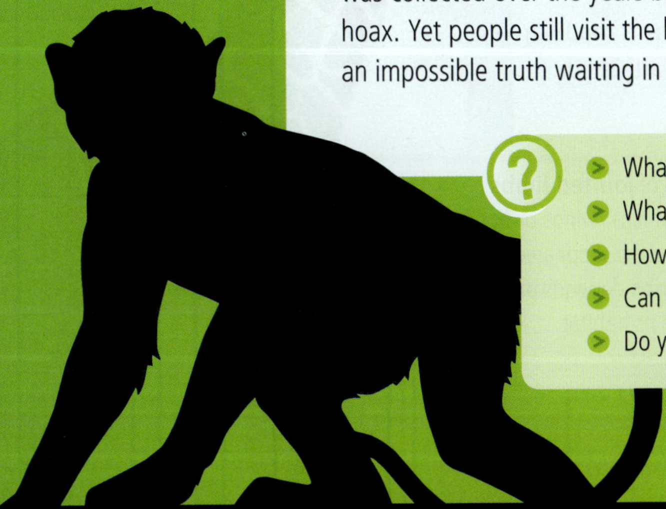

?

- What type of limbs does an aquatic animal have?
- What does an aquatic animal use its limbs for?
- How do aquatic animals breathe?
- Can you name any modern aquatic reptiles?
- Do you think Nessie could be a plesiosaur? Why?

D

E

LOOKING FORWARD >>

- How do vertebrates breathe?
- Which organ helps fish to detect movement and vibration?
- What are the differences between a tadpole and an adult frog?
- Do all reptiles have teeth?
- What characteristics of a bird's body allow it to fly?
- Do mammals lay eggs?
- Which group of mammals do humans belong to?
- What is a bird's beak adapted for?

1 Vertebrates: general characteristics

➲ How do vertebrates breathe?

Vertebrates are multicellular, eukaryotic, heterotrophic organisms that have a **backbone**. The backbone, also called the **spinal column**, is made up of articulated segments of bone known as **vertebrae**.

Vertebrates live in a variety of habitats: terrestrial, aquatic and aerial or arboreal.

1.1 The body structure of a vertebrate

- A vertebrate's body has **bilateral symmetry** and it is generally divided into three parts: **head, trunk** and **tail**.
- The body is covered in **skin** which can have scales, feathers, fur or hair. It can also have different types of associated **glands**, such as poison glands and mammary glands.
- All vertebrate animals have an **internal skeleton** made up of a **skull** and a backbone, to which four limbs are attached.

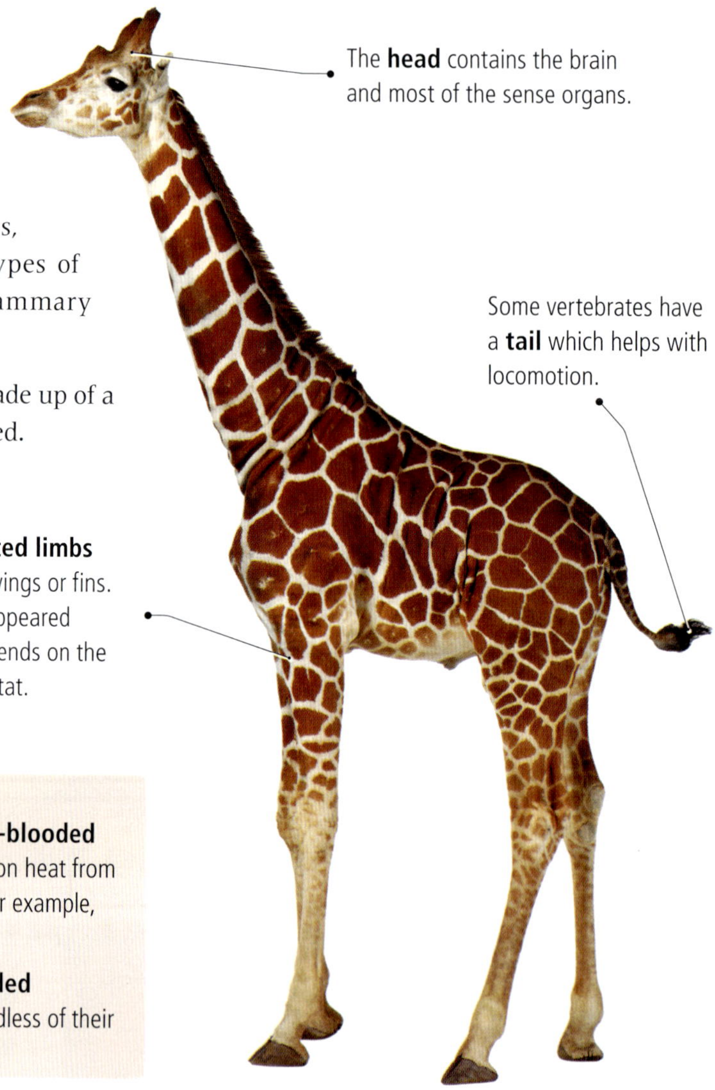

REGULATION OF BODY TEMPERATURE

Fish, amphibians and reptiles are **ectotherms** (also called **cold-blooded** animals). They create very little of their own body heat and rely on heat from their environment to regulate their body temperature. Lizards, for example, bask in the sun to regulate their body temperature.

Birds and mammals are **endotherms** (also called **warm-blooded animals**). They maintain a constant internal temperature, regardless of their environment.

ACTIVITIES

1. Vertebrates have bilateral symmetry. What does this mean? What other types of symmetry are there? Compare the symmetry of vertebrates and invertebrates.
2. What are the differences between endothermic and ectothermic animals? Which group do humans belong to?
3. Give two examples of ectothermic animals. What do they do to regulate their body temperatures?
4. Depending on the characteristics of their limbs, terrestrial vertebrates can be: runners, jumpers, climbers or flyers. Give an example of each type. What characteristics will their limbs have in each case?

1.2 Vital functions of vertebrates

- **Nutrition**. Vertebrates have a complete digestive system. There are herbivores, carnivores, omnivores and also filter-feeders (ducks). Vertebrates breathe through **gills** or **lungs**, depending on whether they live in water or on land. Some species also breathe through their skin. In some organisms, such as frogs, the larvae breathe through gills, whereas the adults do it through lungs.

- **Reproduction**. Vertebrates reproduce **sexually** and most have **separate sexes** (male and female), except for some fish species which are hermaphrodites. In terms of embryo development, vertebrates can be **oviparous** (lay eggs), **ovoviviparous** (the eggs develop inside the mother's body until they are ready to be hatched) or **viviparous** (the embryo develops into a young animal inside the mother's body).

Oviparous. The female lays eggs in the open environment which reduces the chances of survival for the offspring.

Viviparous. The protection of the embryo inside the mother's body increases the chances of survival for the young.

- **Interaction**. A vertebrate's nervous system is made up of a **spinal cord**, which runs along the animal's back, and a highly developed **brain**, located in the head. Vertebrates' sense organs are also highly developed.

CLASSIFYING VERTEBRATES

Fish: vertebrates with gills, scales and fins

Birds: vertebrates with feathers, beaks and wings

Amphibians: vertebrates with a soft skin and four legs

Reptiles: vertebrates with a hard skin covered in scales and four legs

Mammals: vertebrates with four limbs and mammary glands

DID YOU KNOW?

Of all the vertebrates, the **platypus** breaks more 'rules' than any other. It is a mammal, but it lays eggs and has no teats. Milk **seeps** through pores in the mother's skin and collects in folds which the babies drink from. The males are one of the few venomous mammals, able to kill an animal the size of a dog or cause humans terrible pain. They move like reptiles but hunt like dolphins, sensing the electrical activity of their prey when they move. No wonder everyone believed they were fake when they were discovered!

Do you know where platypuses can be found in the world?

ACTIVITIES

5. Explain the main differences between vertebrates and invertebrates.
6. Name four animals that belong to each group of vertebrates.
7. Compare the nervous systems of vertebrates and invertebrates. Which is more developed?

2 Fish

➤ **Which organ helps fish to detect movement and vibration?**

Fish are aquatic animals that live in marine and freshwater environments. They have a **fusiform** body with **fins** that help them to swim. The body is covered in **scales**.

The body of a fish is divided into a head, trunk and tail. The **head** contains the mouth, nostrils, eyes and gills. The **trunk** includes a pair of pectoral fins, a pair of pelvic fins and just one dorsal fin. The **tail** includes the anal fin, the tail fin and the cloaca.

VITAL FUNCTONS OF FISH

- **Nutrition**. Some fish are **carnivores** (salmon, great white shark); others are **herbivores** and eat algae (parrotfish) or **omnivores** (carp). Larvae are usually filter-feeders. Fish breathe through **gills**. These are protected by an **operculum** or **gill cover**.
- **Reproduction**. Fish have **separate sexes**. Most of them are **oviparous** and their **fertilisation** is **external**. Sharks and rays use **internal fertilisation**.
- **Interaction**. Fish have a sense organ called a **lateral line**. This runs along each side of the body and detects changes in water pressure or the presence of prey or predators.

CLASSIFYING FISH

Chondrichthyes (cartilaginous fish), such as rays and sharks have a flexible skeleton of **cartilage**. Their skin is covered in tooth-like scales called **denticles**.

Osteichthyes (bony fish), such as perch, cod and trout, have a rigid bony skeleton. Most have smooth skin with thin transparent scales.

ACTIVITIES

8. Explain the differences between bony fish and cartilaginous fish.
9. What types of fins does a fish have? Make a drawing of a fish and label the fins on it. Look for information on the use of each type of fin.
10. Look for information about how fish are adapted to marine and freshwater environments. Write a short report about this.

3 Amphibians

> What are the differences between a tadpole and an adult frog?

The word *amphibian* comes from Greek and literally means 'both kinds of life'. This is because amphibians can live on land or in water. Some spend most of their lives in water while others are wholly terrestrial and only return to the water for reproduction.

Anurans (**frogs** and **toads**) have no tail in their adult stage. Their hind legs are twice as long as their front legs.

Urodeles (**newts** and **salamanders**) have an elongated body and a tail in their adult stage. Their front and hind legs are the same length.

VITAL FUNCTONS OF AMPHIBIANS

- **Nutrition**. Adults are **carnivores**, whereas larvae are **herbivores**. When amphibians are at their larval stage, they are completely aquatic and breathe through **gills**. When they get to the adult stage, they move onto land and breathe through **lungs** and through their skin.
- **Reproduction**. Amphibians have **separate sexes**. Fertilisation can be **external** (anurans) or **internal** (urodeles). Most of them are **oviparous** and always lay their eggs in water. Most amphibians go through some sort of metamorphosis.

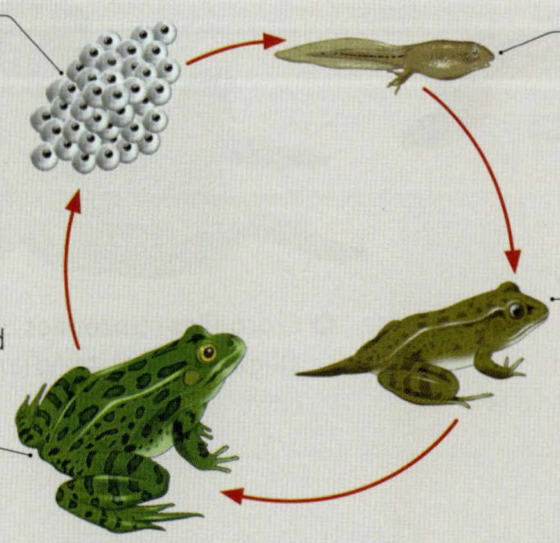

Complete metamorphosis in frogs. Frogs begin their lives as **tadpoles** which hatch from **eggs.** Over time, a tadpole changes and becomes a **froglet**. Eleven weeks after the egg was laid, a fully developed frog emerges from the water. Female frogs lay eggs, males fertilize them, and the whole process begins again.

- **Interaction**. Frogs and toads have vocal chords. They produce sounds that play an important role in their reproduction.

ACTIVITIES

11. Where do amphibians get their name from?

12. Some amphibians have glands that secrete poison. What do you think this poison is used for?

13. Which are more fish-like: tadpoles or froglets? Explain why.

4 Reptiles

Do all reptiles have teeth?

Reptiles were the first vertebrates that completely adapted to living on land. Most reptiles live on land, but turtles, crocodiles, and some snakes live in water. The name *reptile* comes from Latin and means 'creeping or crawling animal'.

VITAL FUNCTONS OF REPTILES

- **Nutrition**. Most reptiles are **carnivorous** predators (crocodile). Some are **herbivores** (tortoises). Most reptiles have teeth. All breathe using **lungs**.
- **Reproduction**. Reptiles have **separate sexes** and **internal fertilisation**. Most reptiles are **oviparous**. Some, such as vipers, are ovoviviparous.

CLASSIFYING REPTILES

Ophidians (**snakes**) have long elongated bodies with no legs.

Chelonians (**tortoises, turtles** and **terrapins**) have a hard beak with no teeth and an external shell.

Lizards (**geckos, iguanas** and **chameleons**) have four legs and a tail.

Crocodiles (**crocodiles, caimans** and **alligators**) have strong jaws and powerful teeth.

ACTIVITIES

14. Explain the similarities and differences between amphibians and reptiles.

15. Dinosaurs, **pterosaurs** and **plesiosaurs** are extinct groups of reptiles that lived on Earth during the secondary era. Look for information on the Internet and explain what environment each of them lived in. What is the environment that most modern reptiles live in?

5 Birds

What characteristics of a bird's body allow it to fly?

Birds are vertebrates with an aerodynamic body and wings, even though not all of them are able to fly.

Birds have a toothless mouth with a corneous **beak**. The beak's shape depends on the bird's diet.

A bird's upper limbs are **wings**.

Birds have a **tail** with feathers.

The lower limbs are **legs**.

A bird's body is covered in **feathers** which help it to fly, maintain body temperature and attract a mate. Bird **bones** are **hollow** and have pockets of air inside them. This makes them lighter so that birds can fly more easily.

VITAL FUNCTONS OF BIRDS

- **Nutrition**. Birds have a wide variety of diets. Their digestive system includes a grinding organ (**gizzard**) where food is ground up. Birds breathe using small **lungs**. These have extensions filled with air (**air sacs**) which help maintain high levels of oxygen-rich air in the respiratory system.
- **Reproduction**. Birds reproduce using **internal fertilisation** and are **oviparous**. They incubate their **hard-shelled eggs** in nests until the chicks are born.
- **Interaction**. Birds have very well developed vision. Some such as owls are able to see very well in the dark. This allows them to hunt at night.

Some birds are **sexually dimorphic**. This means that males and females have very different physical appearances. To attract a mate, birds engage in a **courtship** during which male birds usually sing and exhibit very eye-catching plumage.

Male peacock

CLASSIFYING BIRDS

Ostriches and **penguins** are birds that can't fly.

Anseriformes (**swans**, **ducks** and **geese**) have webbed feet.

Falconiformes (**eagles** and **falcons**) are birds of prey.

Galliformes include **chickens**, **hens**, **peacocks** and **turkeys**.

Ciconiiformes (**flamingos**, **herons** and **storks**) are birds with long necks and legs.

Passerines or 'perching birds' (**robins** and **goldfinches**) include over half of all bird species in the world.

ACTIVITIES

16. Describe the characteristics of bird bones. What are these bones adapted for?

17. Some animals that lack teeth, such as birds, swallow stones. Search for information and find out what the purpose of this is.

6 Mammals

Do mammals lay eggs?

Mammals are vertebrates whose offspring are fed with milk produced by the female's **mammary glands.** Most mammals are terrestrial; some are aquatic (dolphins and whales); and bats are the only mammals that can fly.

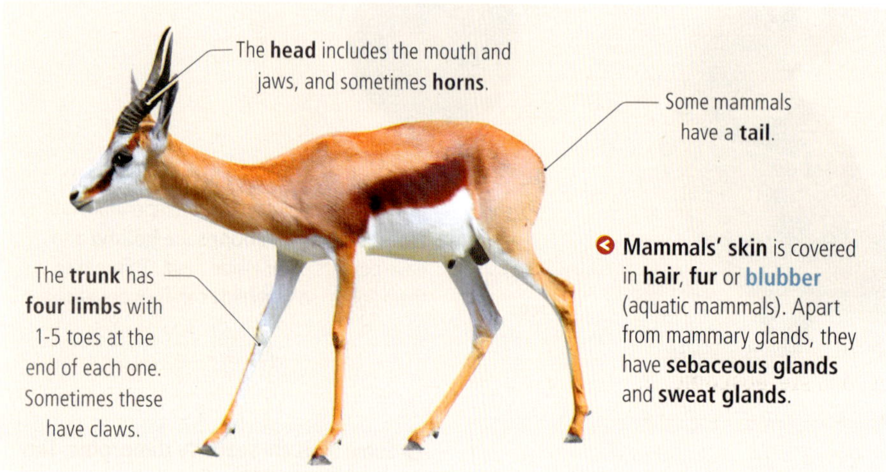

VITAL FUNCTONS OF MAMMALS

- **Nutrition**. Mammals can be carnivores, herbivores or omnivores. They have a digestive system that is specially adapted for their diet. Mammals breathe through highly developed **lungs**.
- **Reproduction**. Mammals reproduce sexually and are sexually dimorphic. Although there are **oviparous** and **ovoviviparous** species, most mammals are **viviparous**.
- **Interaction**. Mammals have the most well-developed nervous system in the animal kingdom.

CLASSIFYING MAMMALS

Monotremes (**echidnas** and **platypuses**) are oviparous.

Marsupials (**kangaroos**, **koalas** and **wallabies**) complete development of the youngs in the mother's **pouch**.

Placentals are viviparous. Most mammals have a **placenta** that nourishes and supplies oxygen to the foetus.

BIG THINKER

Jane Goodall is considered to be the world's foremost expert on chimpanzees – but when she first began to study them she was very unscientific! The **standard** scientific practice at the time was to assign each animal a reference number, but Goodall decided to personalise her subjects. She gave each chimp a unique name that reflected their appearance or personality, like "David Greybeard", the first chimp to approach her. Why do you think Goodall **picked** the name 'David Greybeard'?

ACTIVITIES

18. Explain the differences between:

a. birds and bats **b.** fish and dolphins

19. Look for more information on Jane Goodall and also on Dian Fossey's research on gorillas and write a short report about their work.

7 Diversity of vertebrate animals

Which group of mammals do humans belong to?

Vertebrates are diverse and widespread across the Earth. They are the animals we are most familiar with. Humans are also vertebrates.

HUMANS ARE PRIMATES

Primates are an order of placental mammals that includes monkeys, big apes and humans. The main characteristics of humans are the following:

- Humans have an **upright posture**. We are **plantigrade** (we walk on the soles of our feet) and **bipeds** (we walk on two legs).
- Our arms are shorter than our legs. Our **hands** are **prehensile** due to the presence of a **fully opposable thumb**.
- We have **hair** in large quantities in only some areas, such as the head. There are **sweat glands** all over our bodies.
- Our brain and nervous system are highly developed. We have both eyes at the front of our heads. Our **vision** is **binocular**, in colour and **stereoscopic**. This gives us the ability to see objects in three spacial dimensions: width, height and depth.
- We have a **spoken language** and a long childhood (period of learning).

7.1 How do vertebrates adapt to their environment?

Vertebrates have a wide range of adaptations that allow them to survive, eat, move and reproduce in the habitats where they live.

Camels store fat in their **humps** that can provide energy for up to several weeks. They also store huge amounts of water (up to 46 litres) in their stomachs. This allows them to survive harsh conditions in deserts.

A frog's powerful back legs are adapted for both swimming and jumping.

Predators usually have **sharp teeth**, **claws**, or **beaks** to tear apart their prey.

Reptile and bird eggs are surrounded by a **hard shell** that protects the embryo from predators, damage and drying out.

ACTIVITIES

20. Give examples of biped and quadruped vertebrates. What do you think the advantages of bipedalism are?

21. What diet do humans have? Justify your answer. In reference to the human diet, explain what the following terms mean:

a. vegetarian

b. lacto-vegetarian

c. vegan

22. What function do sweat glands have in mammals?

7.2 Are vertebrates in danger of extinction?

According to recent studies, approximately a fifth of the world's species of vertebrates are facing extinction.

ENDEMIC VERTEBRATES OF THE IBERIAN PENINSULA

Aphanius iberus is an endemic species of fish whose risk of extinction is one of the greatest of any Iberian vertebrate.

The Iberian frog *(Rana Iberica)* is mostly restricted to the northwestern area of the Peninsula.

The Seoane's viper *(Vipera seoanei)* is a venomous species endemic to northern Spain.

The Iberian imperial eagle is an endangered species that lives only in a few areas of Spain.

The Cantabrian capercaillie *(Tetrao urogallus cantabricus)* is an endangered species which is illegal to hunt.

The Iberian lynx *(Lynx pardinus)* exists only in the wild in some areas of southern Spain. It is the world's most threatened species of felid.

ACTIVITIES

23. Look for information about the following vertebrates that are endemic to the Iberian Peninsula. Write a short report about them, including information on: the group of vertebrates each of them belongs to, their distribution area, and whether they are endangered or not.

a. the Mediterranean monk seal
b. the Hierro giant lizard
c. the Pyrenean desman
d. the toothcarp (*Valencia hispanica*)
e. the Cantabrian brown bear

24. Speaking about extinction, a professor and ecologist at Harvard University once said:

"The backbone of biodiversity is being eroded."

Which group of organisms do you think this statement referred to? Explain why.

Discovery techniques

What is a bird's beak adapted for?

Identifying birds by their beaks

Have you ever wondered why birds have so many different shapes of beaks?

Birds' beaks have been adapted for their diverse feeding habits. This makes it easy to identify birds just by looking at their beaks. It also makes it possible to find out what each type of bird eats.

Chisel-like beak for **drilling** holes in wood to look for insects.

Woodpecker

Spear-like beak for fishing

Kingfisher

Shredder-like beak for capturing and **tearing apart** prey.

Eagle

Needle-like beak for extracting nectar from flowers

Hummingbird

Cracking beak for cracking the hard shell of nuts and seeds.

Sparrow

Strainer-like beak for **straining** insects and plants out of water and mud

Duck

ACTIVITIES

1. Decide whether the birds in the key above are carnivores, herbivores or omnivores. Which of them are predators?
2. What type of beak from the key above do birds of prey, such as owls, have? What about herons?
3. Similar to the shape of a bird's beak, the shape of a bird's feet also helps us identify and classify the bird. Look for information about this topic and, with a classmate, write a key to classify birds according to this criterion.
   a. Do a drawing of each type of feet.
   b. Give at least one example of a bird of each type.
   c. What is the shape of a bird's feet related to?

Revision activities

1. Describe the three main parts of a vertebrate body and an invertebrate body. Draw an example from each group to compare them.

2. Vertebrates have an internal skeleton. With a partner, fill in the chart with information about the advantages and disadvantages of internal skeletons and exoskeletons. Then, discuss which one you think is better suited for arboreal, aerial, aquatic and terrestrial environments.

	advantages	disadvantages
internal skeleton		
exoskeleton		

3. Give some examples of filter-feeding vertebrates. Why is it important to keep their water supply clean?

4. Name the vertebrates that lay eggs. Then, discuss the following questions with a partner:
   a. Why do frogs and other amphibians lay so many eggs?
   b. What could this be related to?

5. From analysing fossils, it was discovered that fish were the first vertebrates to appear on Earth. These early fish had no jaws, but later fish developed them. Name two types of fish that are now famous for their powerful jaws. What do they use their jaws for?

6. 'Living fossil' is a term coined by Charles Darwin to describe creatures that have remained much the same for millions of years.
   a. Search for information about these so-called living fossils and name five of them.
   b. Choose one of them and write a short report about it.

7. Label the type of fish in the photos and explain the differences between them.

A

B

8. What happens if the lateral line in a fish is damaged?

9. Bony fish tend to fossilize better than other fish or birds. Reflecting on what you know about the bones and structures of these organisms, why do you think this is?

10. Most bony fish have a swim bladder, which allows them to float. Swim bladder disease, which causes fish to sink or float upside down, is a common problem in aquarium fish. Do some research on the disease and write a short report about it. Why do you think this is more common in aquarium fish than in those that live in the wild?

11. Both fish and mammals need oxygen to breathe. Compare respiration in fish and in mammals.

12. Decide whether the following sentence is true or false. Justify your answer.

    Amphibians are vertebrates with four legs and a hard skin covered in scales.

13. Give two examples of adaptations by amphibians for movement on land.

14. A large proportion of amphibians – some researchers say 35% – are endangered. What is it about amphibians that makes them sensitive to changes in the environment?

15. Explain the process of metamorphosis in frogs. Is it complete or incomplete? Explain why.

16. Lizards and snakes are both reptiles, but they have many differences. Look for information and explain the similarities and differences between lizards and snakes by completing the chart below. Add your own category at the end.

	lizards	snakes
nutrition		
reproduction		
endotherms or ectotherms		
legs or no legs		
eyelid		
ear opening		
tail regeneration		
forked tongue		
...		

17. Which era was known as the 'age of reptiles'? Search for information to explain the reasons for this.

18. What characteristic of reptiles allows them to thrive in arid environments? Search for information and give two examples of such species.

19 Say whether the following sentence is true or false. If it is false, explain why:

Birds and insects are related because both have wings and can fly.

20 Parent birds usually care for their eggs and offspring.

a. Why is this care necessary?
b. Name other vertebrates that care a lot for their young.

21 While no birds are known to release venom, there are a few bird species that have poisonous substances on their skin. This makes the birds dangerous to eat. Search for more information on toxic birds. Write up a short report based on your findings. Make sure to include information on the illness coturnism.

22 Search on the Internet for information about the fossil Archaeopteryx. Explain why it was an important discovery.

23 The dodo was a species of bird that became extinct in the 1600s. Do some research on the dodo and write a short report to explain why it became extinct.

24 Match the following words with their corresponding functions.

blubber, cartilage, denticles, feathers, gills, gizzard, lateral line, mammary glands, operculum, placenta, spinal column, sweat glands

a. An organ that supplies oxygen to the foetus.
b. A thick layer of fat under the skin that is used for insulation.
c. A part of the skin that regulates body temperature.
d. An organ that grinds up food to aid digestion.
e. These help certain species to find a mate.
f. A respiratory organ in some vertebrates.
g. Tooth-like scales.
h. An organ that surrounds and protects the spinal cord.
i. An organ that produces milk to feed its offspring.
j. A flap that covers a gill.
k. A sense organ that runs along each side of the body and detects changes.
l. A flexible skeleton.

25 Give one example of an organism that has each type of the features in Activity 24.

26 A unique bird from Africa, the shoe-billed stork, has a beak shaped like a shoe! Think back to what you know about beak shapes and functions. What do you think the shoebill uses its beak for?

27 The two classes of vertebrates that are covered in scales are also ectotherms. First, say which classes of vertebrates have scales. Second, think of a reason why having scales may be related to being cold-blooded

28 Decide whether the following sentence is true or false. Give reasons for your answer.

All mammals are ectotherms and are covered in hair or fur.

29 Officially, the number of bones in the human body is 206. But does every human have the same number of bones? Search for information to explain why or why not.

30 If an animal does not have skin, can it be a mammal? Explain why or why not.

31 Decide whether the following sentence is true or false. Give reasons to support your answer.

Humans and other mammals have an average body temperature lower than that of their surroundings.

32 Give examples of three terrestrial mammals and three aquatic mammals. Then, say which of these are endotherms and which are ectotherms.

33 Discuss with a partner whether the following statement is true or false. Then look for information to check your answer.

Bipedalism in humans helped free up the use of their hands so they could use tools.

34 Explain the similarities and differences between birds and mammals

35 Would you classify rats and mice as marsupials, monotremes or placental mammals? Explain your answer.

36 Search for information about Louis and Mary Leakey and explain why their research is so important.

Read and think

WHY DON'T THE ANIMALS THAT LIVE AT THE POLES FREEZE?

The North and South Poles are the coldest places on Earth. They are completely covered in snow and ice for most of the year. No ectothermic animals (amphibians and reptiles) inhabit the Poles because they could not survive in the extremely low temperatures. With temperatures of around 4 °C, their nervous system would stop functioning, their body would shut down and the organisms would eventually die.

Endothermic vertebrates (birds and mammals) are much better suited to **withstanding** very cold temperatures, but they must use up a large amount of energy in doing so. However, not all mammals and birds can endure the low temperatures found at the Poles. The animals that can survive at the Poles do not freeze to death because their bodies have adapted to the low temperatures. In other cases, there are behavioural adaptations.

Foxes and **wolves** have a thick layer of body fat and a thick fur coat, which help them to conserve their body heat.

To avoid losing their body heat, **musk oxen** have two layers of woolly hair that almost completely covers their bodies.

Walruses, **seals** and **whales** survive thanks to a thick layer of fat under their skin (**blubber**) that acts as an insulator.

The **brown lemming**, a small rodent that lives in the Arctic, stays warm in tunnels under the snow until the summer comes.

Feathers keep the **snowy owl** warm. It stays still when the temperature drops to avoid using up its heat energy.

Apart from their anatomical adaptations, **penguins** huddle together to keep warm in freezing Antarctic temperatures.

Some vertebrates, such as some species of birds and whales, are only part-time residents in Polar regions. They spend the summer in northern regions and migrate to warmer, lower latitudes during the winter months.

ANSWER THE QUESTIONS

1. What types of animals are found in the Earth's polar regions: ectotherms or endotherms? Justify your answer
2. What adaptions have animals that live in the polar regions developed?
3. Why do you think many of the animals that live at the Poles hibernate?
4. Describe animal adaptations to deserts. Are they the same or different to the adaptations to cold areas?

Work it out

CONCEPT MAP

Use the words in the word cloud to create your own unit map in your notebook. Write any connecting texts you need.

placentals humans fish ciconiiformes amphibians chondrichthyes big apes anseriformes galliformes primates birds vertebrates osteichthyes marsupials anurans passerines ophidians crocodiles ostriches and penguins mammals monkeys chelonians lizards monotremes falconiformes reptiles urodeles

SELF-ASSESSMENT

Carry out a self-assessment of what you learned in this unit. Choose one answer for each question and then check your answers.

1. A vertebrate's body has …
   - a. bilateral symmetry, a backbone and an exoskeleton.
   - b. bilateral symmetry and an endoskeleton.
   - c. a backbone and a lack of symmetry.
2. The lateral line in fish …
   - a. is covered in scales.
   - b. helps them swim.
   - c. detects pressure and movement.
3. Which animals breathe through their gills?
   - a. Tadpoles and fish
   - b. Fish and frogs
   - c. Tadpoles and froglets
4. All reptiles …
   - a. breathe using lungs.
   - b. have a hard beak instead of teeth.
   - c. have four legs
5. Which of the following have a body covered in scales?
   - a. Reptiles
   - b. Amphibians
   - c. Mammals
6. Birds are the only animals that …
   - a. are able to fly.
   - b. are endotherms.
   - c. have feathers.
7. Both reptiles and birds …
   - a. are oviparous and incubate their eggs.
   - b. are endotherms.
   - c. have four legs.
8. Marsupials …
   - a. don't have mammary glands.
   - b. are placental mammals.
   - c. are a group of mammals.
9. Mammals …
   - a. have bipedal locomotion.
   - b. are always viviparous.
   - c. breathe through their lungs.
10. Humans …
    - a. have sweat glands and hair.
    - b. have a short period of development.
    - c. aren't vertebrates.

Glossary

A

arboreal (adj): related to trees; of or living in trees

attached (adj): joined to something

attempt (n): the act of trying to do something, especially something difficult

average (n): a number calculated by adding several amounts together, finding a total, and dividing the total by the number of amounts

B

barnacle (n): a marine crustacean with an external shell, which attaches itself to a variety of surfaces, typically to boat hulls and wharves or jetties

beehive (n): a structure in which bees are kept in order to harvest their honey

binocular vision (adj): involving or using both eyes

blood clot (n): a solid lump of blood that is formed in a blood vessel

blubber (n): a thick insulating layer of fatty tissue below the skin of aquatic mammals such as whales and seals

brightly-coloured (adj): with colours that are strong and easy to see

bristle (n): any short stiff hair of an animal or plant

buttermilk (n): the liquid that remains after butter has been separated from milk

C

chisel-like (adj): with the form of a hand tool made up of a flat steel blade with a cutting edge attached to a handle

clone (n): a plant or animal that has the same genes as the original from which it was produced

courtship (n): the behaviour of male birds and other animals aimed at attracting a mate

corneous (adj): made out of a substance similar to that of horns or antlers

covering (n): a layer of something that covers something else

culture dish (n): a shallow, circular, transparent dish used in laboratories, especially for producing cultures of microorganisms

cultured (adj): grown in an artificial medium

curdle (v): to turn into a soft, white substance formed when milk coagulates

cuttlefish (n): a sea animal with eight arms, two tentacles and a wide flat shell inside its body, that produces ink when it is attacked

D

decaying (adj): rotting; decomposing

devastating (adj): extremely destructive

drill (v): to make a hole in (something)

E

engulf (v): to completely surround and cover something or someone

F

fishery (n): a fishing area where fish are caught

fuel (n): any material that produces heat or power, usually when it is burnt

fulfil (v): to bring about the completion or achievement of something

fusiform (adj): elongated, wider in the middle than at both ends

H

harness (v): to control and make use of something

hierarchical (adj): of the nature of a hierarchy; arranged in order of rank

I

inoculate (v): to introduce a substance or organism into another substance or organism

L

latch onto (v): to become attached to somebody/something

limb (n): appendage of an animal such as an arm, leg, wing or fin

lobed (adj): rounded in shape, usually found in a group, forming a larger structure

locust (n): a large and mainly tropical grasshopper which migrates in vast swarms that cause extensive damage to crops

louse (plural form: lice)(n): a small insect that lives on the bodies or in the hair of humans and animals

M

maintenance (n): the process of preserving a condition

mate (v): to pair a male animal and a female animal for reproduction

mimicry (n): the resemblance shown by one animal species to another, which protects them from predators

moisture (n): a small amount of a liquid (water) that can make something wet

moult (v): (animal) to lose skin, fur, feathers, etc. as a natural process so that new skin, etc. can grow

N

naked eye (n): unassisted vision; without a telescope, microscope, or other device

needle (n): a thin, hard, pointed leaf

nettle (n): a wild plant with heart-shaped leaves that are covered in hairs that sting

P

passageway (n): a tube in the body through which air or liquid passes

pest (n): a destructive insect or other animal that attacks crops, food, livestock, etc.

pick (a name) (v): to choose or select

pigment (n): a substance that exists naturally in animals and plants and gives their skin, leaves, etc. a particular colour

plesiosaur (n): an extinct marine reptile of the Jurassic and Cretaceous periods with a long neck, short tail, and paddle-like limbs

poultry (n): farmyard birds such as hens, ducks, geese and turkeys

prehensile (adj): an animal's limb or tail that is capable of grasping

prolific (adj): a plant, animal, or person producing many offspring

pterosaur (n): an extinct flying reptile of the Jurassic and Cretaceous periods with membranous wings supported by a very long fourth finger

puppy (n): a young dog

R

regenerate (v): to grow after loss or damage

release (v): to give freedom or free movement to something

replace (v): to provide a substitute for something that has been lost

resemble (v): to have a similar appearance to or qualities in common with someone or something

reveal (v): to make something known or to show something that is surprising or that was previously unknown

revival (n): a renewed use or interest in past customs or practices

rudimentary (adj): basic; not elaborate or perfected

S

scale (n): BIOLOGY one of the small, flat pieces that cover the skin of fish and reptiles

scavenger (n): an animal that feeds on carrion, dead plant material, or refuse

seep (v): the action of a liquid flowing or leaking slowly through porous material or small holes

segmented (adj): divided into or composed of segments or sections

sessile (adj): (an organism) fixed in one place; immobile

shade (n): an area that is dark and cool where sunlight cannot reach

shelter (n): a shielded or safe place; protection

shredder-like (adj): with the form of a machine that is used for cutting things into small pieces

slightly (adv): to a small extent

spear-like (adj): with the form of a weapon with a pointed tip, and a long shaft that is used for thrusting or throwing

specimen (n): a single example of an animal or a plant

spikes (n): sharp-pointed objects or structures growing out of an animal or a plant

spore (n): a miniscule, typically one-celled, reproductive unit capable of giving rise to a new individual without sexual fusion, characteristic of lower plants, fungi, and protozoans

standard (adj): the usual or accepted kind

starch (n): an odourless, tasteless white substance occurring widely in plant tissue and obtained chiefly from cereals and potatoes

steroids (n): chemical substances produced naturally in the body that can sometimes be used to treat various diseases

stinging (adj): animals or plants that inflict wounds on other organisms by injecting poison or venom

strain (v): to pour or pass a substance through a sieve or filter

succulent (n): a plant that is able to exist in dry conditions by using water stored in its tissues

sucker (n): a flat or concave organ enabling an animal to cling to a surface by suction

T

thickener (n): a substance that is used to make a liquid more viscous

thickness (n): the distance between the top and bottom or front and back surfaces of something

tick (n): a small insect that lives on and sucks the blood of other animals

tiny (adj): very small in size or amount

U

uneven (adj): not level, equal, flat, or continuous

unfertilised (adj): an egg cell that has not been fecundated

upright (adj): vertical or erect

V

viable (adj): BIOLOGY a plant, animal, or cell capable of surviving or living successfully

viscous (adj): thick and sticky and that does not flow easily

W

widespread (adj): extending over a wide area

withstand (v): to stand up to forcefully; to resist

Big thinkers

Name: Carl Linnaeus

Lived: 1707–1778

Nationality: Swedish

Interests: Botany, biology, zoology

Bright ideas: He laid the foundations for the modern biological naming scheme of binomial nomenclature. He is known as the father of modern taxonomy, and is also considered one of the fathers of modern ecology.

Name: Alexander Fleming

Lived: 1881–1955

Nationality: Scottish

Interests: Bacteriology, pharmacology, immunology

Bright ideas: His best-known discoveries are the enzyme lysozyme in 1923 and the antibiotic substance penicillin in 1928. He was elected Fellow of the Royal Society in 1943 and knighted in 1944.

Name: Anna Atkins

Lived: 1799–1871

Nationality: English

Interests: Botany, photography

Bright ideas: Atkins is known to have had access to a camera as early as 1841 and some people say that she was the first female photographer. She also illustrated a book about shells, translated by her father.

Name: Charles Darwin

Lived: 1809–1882

Nationality: English

Interests: Natural history, geology

Bright ideas: He is best known for his contributions to evolutionary theory. He established that all species of living things have descended over time from common ancestors. Also, together with Alfred Russel Wallace, he introduced his scientific theory that the branching pattern of evolution resulted from a process that he called 'natural selection'.

Name: Jane Goodall

Lived: 1934–…

Nationality: English

Interests: Anthropology, ethology, primatology

Bright ideas: She is considered to be the world's foremost expert on chimpanzees. Goodall is best known for her 55-year study of social and family interactions of wild chimpanzees in the Gombe Stream National Park, Tanzania. She has also worked extensively on conservation and animal welfare issues.

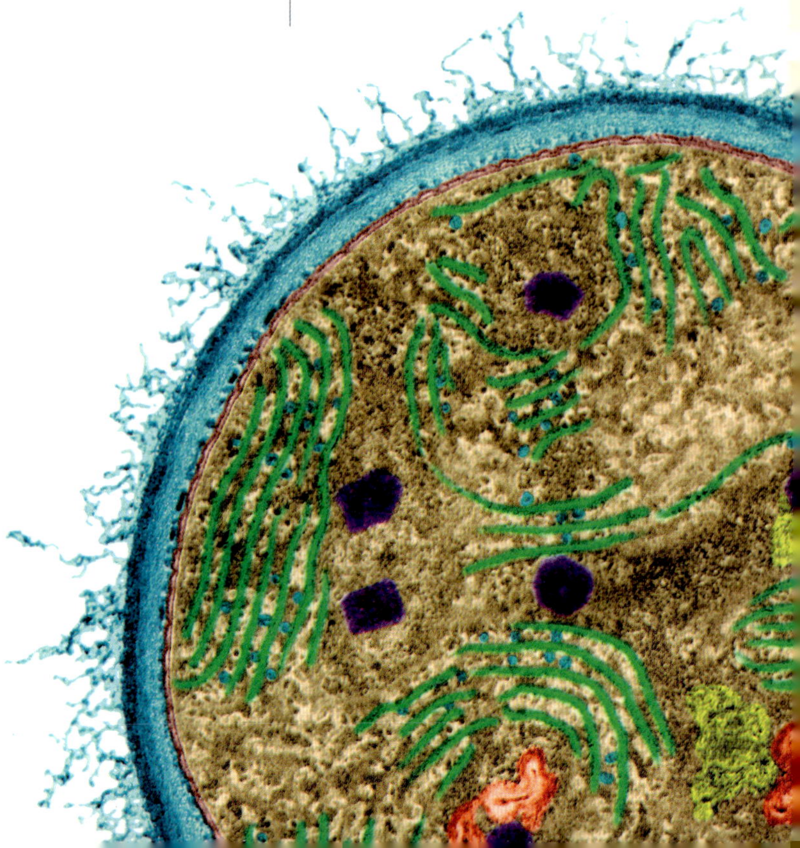